The Political Thought of Abdullah Öcalan

The Political Thought of Abdullah Öcalan

Kurdistan, Woman's Revolution and Democratic Confederalism

PlutoPress
www.plutobooks.com

International Initiative Edition

First published 2017 by Pluto Press
345 Archway Road, London N6 5AA

www.plutobooks.com

Translated by Havin Guneser and International Initiative 'Freedom for
Abdullah Öcalan – Peace In Kurdistan'
www.ocalan-books.com

British Library Cataloguing in Publication Data
A catalogue record for this book is available from the British Library

ISBN   978 0 7453 9976 8   Paperback
ISBN   978 1 7868 0087 9   PDF eBook
ISBN   978 1 7868 0089 3   Kindle eBook
ISBN   978 1 7868 0088 6   EPUB eBook

This book is printed on paper suitable for recycling and made from fully
managed and sustained forest sources. Logging, pulping and manufacturing
processes are expected to conform to the environmental standards of the
country of origin.

Typeset by Stanford DTP Services, Northampton, England

Simultaneously printed in the United Kingdom and United States of America

Contents

Foreword

Nadje Al-Ali

THE CONTEXT OF READING
ABDULLAH ÖCALAN TODAY

For many of us around the world, the historical juncture unfolding is very frightening indeed. We are faced with multiple existential challenges – ranging from violent wars and conflicts, particularly in Africa and in the Middle East, as well as an ongoing large forced displacement of people from war zones, but increasingly also due to devastating environmental damage and climate change. Meanwhile, fascism is on the rise again, most notably in the form of *Daesh* or ISIS, the so-called Islamic State, as well as right-wing governments and movements promoting racism, Islamophobia and anti-immigration/anti-refugee sentiments and mobilisations in Europe, the US and other places around the globe. Many of us are rethinking the meaning of democracy at a time when anti-intellectualism, populism, outright distortions and lies appear to not only have gained credibility but also increasing authority.

Those of us who have been invested in various struggles and causes linked to social justice, equality, and a fairer distribution of resources have also frequently been involved in discussions and practices, trying to find more participatory and democratic ways of decision-making and engaging in politics. Personally, as a feminist academic and activist, the question of how to do politics has been as important as the actual content of feminist politics. Despite the existence of exciting and inspiring social movements and political struggles around the world that have tried to apply more horizontal ways of decision-making, the current global social, political and economic crises fill many people with horror and sadness. We seem to have reached a dangerous tipping point, when populations everywhere are extremely polarised, when nationalist and essentialist identity politics are on the rise, and when the scapegoating of religious, ethnic and sexual minorities is being normalised yet again. Speaking truth to power has become increasingly rare and in numerous contexts, a very risky, if not life-threatening, act.

Looking specifically to the Middle East, the region I am most familiar with through my research and activism, the situation seems to be particularly dire. The enormous hope and joy evoked by the revolutionary processes, protest movements and creative acts of resistance against the various authoritarian regimes in the region appears to have been replaced by fear and despair. This is due to a rise in violent repression of any form of dissent, escalating sectarian tensions and conflicts, the continuing militarisation of politics, the ongoing neoliberalisation of economies, in addition to the growth and expansion of radical Islamist ideology, whether in the form of established political parties and regimes or militant groups. However, I agree with those commentators who note that any revolutionary processes and radical transformations in the region require long-term commitment and analytical lenses, and not all is lost even if it might appear like that. There is a critical mass of people in the Middle East and within its diasporas who do wish for freedom, equality and democracy. But their aspirations, visions and efforts are too often brutally repressed by current governments and by fiercely conservative social and political constituencies.

It is in the context of seeking out those voices, activists, organisations and movements in the region that pursue radical and creative ideas and practices of democracy, freedom and social justice that I began to get more and more interested in the Kurdish political movement. My feminist instincts and curiosity led me to try to understand the ideas and history behind the all too often superficial and glossy representations of attractive female Kurdish fighters engaged in armed conflict with ISIS militants in Kobanê and elsewhere in northern Syria (the area also referred to as Rojava). I was puzzled by the contradiction of the glorifying narratives and accounts of the female fighters while the Kurdistan Workers Party (PKK) continues to be criminalised in many contexts and accounts.

From readings and conversations, I was aware that one of the major ideological and political underpinnings of the Kurdish resistance to ISIS in northern Syria, northern Iraq and Sinjar (Shengal), was rooted in the political experiences and ideas linked to the PKK. I was also curious to understand why the Kurdish political movement in Turkey (northern Kurdistan), particularly the women's movement, would be so different from the Kurdish women's movement in the Kurdistan Region of Iraq (KRI), that is southern Kurdistan, a region I had known over a longer period through research and travel. Kurdish women's organisations in the KRI seemed to be challenged by far more conservative gender norms and relations propagated by their political leadership. And aside from a few outstanding exceptions, Kurdish women's rights activists in the KRI tend to be more neoliberal in their interpretations and practices of feminism, often focusing on women's leadership and empowerment as conceptualised by international funders and NGOs.

It is through my collaborative ethnographic research over the last two years with my colleague at SOAS, Dr Latif Tas, that I became more and more interested in the relationship between the political development of the Kurdish movement, particularly the women's movement, and the ideas of Abdullah Öcalan, the imprisoned leader not only of the PKK but a much wider Kurdish political movement in Turkey (northern Kurdistan) and beyond. My encounters, conversations and interviews with Kurdish women's rights activists in Turkey and in the diaspora, MPs belonging to the multi-ethnic, progressive People's Democratic Party (HDP), co-mayors, journalists and academics were humbling and profoundly inspiring. On several occasions, it was mind boggling for me to hear Kurdish women's rights activists tell us that nationalism was bad for women, whether Turkish nationalism or Kurdish nationalism. These were activists who were part of a large ethnic minority that had been systematically marginalised and deprived of basic cultural and political rights in Turkey, such as Kurdish language teaching in schools. I was genuinely puzzled that they were not advocating for an independent Kurdish nation state but for more democracy and recognition within Turkey.

While the activists and MPs we talked to were clearly drawing on their own experiences as women within a wider political movement, they all referred to the prison writings of Abdullah Öcalan as highly influential, transformative and instrumental in shaping their political ideas and struggle. As a social anthropologist specialising in women and gender issues within the Middle East and its diasporas, I tend to focus less on texts, but more on the ways in which texts and ideas are being interpreted, negotiated, implemented and contested by people. But there came a point in our enquiry when it was obvious to me that I had to engage with the writings and ideas of Öcalan, in order to better understand the ideas, attitudes and practices of the Kurdish women and men we were talking to.

Let me make it absolutely clear: I have not studied Abdullah Öcalan's prison writings (he has been in prison for over 18 years now) carefully over the years, as many of my peers and colleagues have done. Nor am I an expert in the various intellectual and philosophical underpinnings of his work. Initially influenced by Marxist-Leninist thought, in his more recent writings, as many commentators have illustrated, Öcalan has been particularly stimulated by Murray Bookchin, the American anarchist and social ecologist. Other influential thinkers and movements often quoted include the American anarchist Emma Goldman, Immanuel Wallerstein, V. Gordon Childe, Fernand Braudel, Friedrich Nietzsche, Michel Foucault, the Frankfurt School and the Zapatistas.

To be quite frank, for a long time I was very sceptical about what I perceived to be another male über-patriarch whose picture seemed to pop up everywhere. If anything, I was slightly taken aback by his cult-like status. But my initial scepticism and reluctance to engage was replaced by a great sense of appreciation, respect, and excitement. I have come to recognise Abdullah Öcalan not only as a political leader who has been able to engage in self-criticism and change his positions radically, but also as a political philosopher and inspiring civic rights figure.

BETWEEN THEORY AND PRACTICE

Most inspiring for me is the fact that we have a male political leader who started an armed militia who recognises that armed struggle and violence are not the most effective and preferred means to engage in politics and to obtain peace. He leaves no doubt that the wish for peace and for laying down arms is high on the agenda. But he also reminds us that people need to have a sense of hope and trust to be able to actually lay down their arms completely.

Even more astonishing from my perspective is the fact that this male leader does not tell women to wait their turn, as historically and cross culturally has been the case, over and over again. In many revolutionary and liberation struggles, women were told to put aside their specific concerns, support the wider struggle and their menfolk: their claims would be addressed when the time was ripe. Only the time was never right. Whether in Vietnam, Eritrea, Algeria or Palestine, women experienced backlashes and had to learn the hard way that revolutions and national liberations tend to marginalise women and their specific concerns.

Having moved away from the initial main political goal to obtain an independent Kurdistan, Öcalan still holds that the right to self-determination includes the right to a nation-state. However, in a radical shift from his previous position, he now argues that the establishment of an independent nation-state does not increase the freedom of a people. In contrast, the state, in his view, is a source of much suffering and oppression in different contexts. This is largely because capitalism and patriarchy find their optimum expression within the nation-state and, in turn, shape its structure and fabric. For Öcalan, sexism is one of the main pillars of the nation-state, which, of course, has been an argument also made by many feminist scholars and activists.

Despite his clearly negative assessment of the nation-state, he does not advocate for its dismantling, but proposes a model of governance that diminishes its power while increasing the power of citizens. The idea is to pursue radical and participatory democracy within the boundaries of existing nation-states through federation and self-organisation. Yet, what I find particularly appealing about his proposed model at this historical moment is the fact that democracy is not simply conceived of in terms of participation and horizontal decision-making. We know from many different examples across the world, that majority rule and street politics do not necessarily uphold democratic principles and egalitarian values. Simple majoritarianism can easily lead to populism, which in turn might lead to fascism and the oppression of ethnic, religious and sexual minorities, women, the poor, and the socially marginalised. Yet, the aim of what is coined democratic confederalism is to provide a democratic and egalitarian framework for all people, including minorities, and specific social groups, particularly women, to have autonomy and to be able to organize freely. The ideological pillars of this consensus-oriented and multicultural political framework are ecology, more specifically a commitment to preserve the environment, as well as feminism, that is, a commitment to gender equality and justice. A more equal distribution of resources continues to be central to Öcalan's thinking.

Admittedly, the ideas, however appealing, might sound utopian and unrealistic, given our global and national forms of governance in general, and the specific conditions within the Middle East in particular. However, the Kurdish political movement has been engaged in the interpretation, translation and implementation of Öcalan's vision and ideas in different contexts over the last few years. Most visibly and successfully, we have seen the idea of democratic confederalism being pursued in practice in northern Syria. Since 2003, the Democratic Union Party (PYD), which, although a separate political entity, shares ideological roots in the PKK, began to organise in Rojava and by 2005 started to pursue key ideas more practically, even if clandestinely. More recently, the Movement for a Democratic Society (*Tevgera Civaka Demokratik* or TEV-DEM) has been established as an umbrella organisation to pursue the vision of democratic confederalism at the same time as Kurds in northern Syria have been involved in an armed struggle against ISIS, while also being under attack by a number of other armed groups, along with the Turkish military.

It is beyond the scope of this foreword to go into details of what has been unfolding in northern Syria. Several scholars and activists have written about it already; see for example, the recently published *Revolution in Rojava: Democratic Autonomy and Women's Liberation in Syrian Kurdistan*, by Michael Knapp, Anja Flach and Ercan Ayboğa (2016). It remains to be seen whether this unique social and political experiment of an egalitarian society will achieve its goals and will be given a chance to develop, flourish and possibly expand, or whether it will be crushed due to local, regional and international power games. While Kurds have constituted the most effective resistance to ISIS in northern Syria and also in Iraq, we know that this might not translate into more long-term alliances and support. Interests are complex and friendships fragile when it comes to the struggle over territory, power and resources in the region.

What I can discuss with more certainty, given my own research, are the attempts of implementing aspects of radical democracy in the context of Turkey, especially those linked to women's involvement in politics. Prior to engaging in collaborative research on the gendered dimensions of the Turkish–Kurdish conflict, I had read about the system of co-chairing between women and men in all political leadership positions. Initially I was very sceptical, as I saw the risks of quota systems applied in other contexts of the Middle East: they tend to be more of a cosmetic exercise as opposed to a means to redress inequalities. Often not implemented consistently, quotas tend to put female relatives or friends of conservative political leaders into power positions without challenging the overall system of gender imbalance. I was therefore very surprised to see that in the context of the Kurdish political movement in Turkey, and also in relation to the progressive Kurdish-led but multi-ethnic and multicultural People's Democratic Party (HDP), co-chairing was taken seriously. Not only are women involved in all aspects of decision-making across all positions, whether at local or national level, at the level of MPs or mayors, but the system also tries to involve youth and religious and ethnic minorities other than Kurds.

Clearly there are tensions and problems that will require discussion, reflection, shifts in practice and long-term commitment. Not surprisingly, there is still a big gap between the way the Kurdish political leadership and activists in the movement talk about and practise politics, and the way many men and women in the wider Kurdish community do. Noticeably, conservative gender norms and relations continue to be widespread and deeply ingrained despite the practices and the official rhetoric of the movement as well as Öcalan's writings.

Kurdish communities are also not entirely immune to increasing Islamist militancy, whether in the form of Kurdish Hizbullah or ISIS. Yet, the hard work and long-term commitment of Kurdish women's rights activists is paying off in many ways and is starting to transform not only the way that men in the political movement think but also the wider community. Young women are more confident in their ability to get involved in decision-making and politics, and many more women are working in a different range of jobs. Several of the women's rights activists we talked to stressed that their achievements were not merely a matter of rights being handed to them on a platter, i.e. because Öcalan said so, but that they had to fight for them step by step over many years. Öcalan himself would have been aware of and influenced by the struggle of Kurdish women's rights activists and would have recognised that they were struggling not merely against the Turkish state but also patriarchal norms within the Kurdish community, including the political movement. This requires us to look at Öcalan's writing and the development of the Kurdish political and women's movement in a much more dialectical way than what is often done.

Another obvious gap between the ideas of Öcalan and those of many Kurds is that the notion of an independent Kurdistan continues to have much currency. This is understandable in a context where the Turkish state has been cracking down brutally on Kurdish towns and communities after several failed attempts at peace negotiations.

Sadly, many of the Kurdish women and men we interviewed for our research, who have been active proponents of peace and democracy, and of pursuing political channels as opposed to armed struggle, have been arrested and imprisoned as part of the wide-scale purge and crack down following the failed coup in July 2016.

During our interviews, it became obvious that the issue of sexuality has remained a taboo, even if Öcalan has addressed it in some of his writings outside this book. I understand that due to historical and ongoing current cultural and social norms and pressures, it has not been possible to address conservative gender norms in relation to sexuality. Looking forward, however, I wonder whether it is possible to be part of a more egalitarian society without becoming sexless beings as seems to be required at least in the context of the armed branch of the Kurdish movement. Given prevailing notions about women's honour and the fear of shaming the community through women's conduct, it is understandable that sexuality has been bracketed off the discourse about women's liberation. However, as long as sexuality is considered a taboo, there is a risk that we see the emergence of two separate communities: an egalitarian one of sexless militants and activists, and ordinary communities in which reproduction will continue and notions of honour and shame will circumscribe women's lives.

Another issue that might require further probing is the idea of *jineolojî* as a paradigm shifting new science of women as conceptualised by Öcalan. In my reading, this idea appears to ignore the long history of feminists across the world who, alongside other thinkers linked to Marxist, poststructuralist and postcolonial epistemologies, have critiqued scientific positivism, the androcentric and ethnocentric nature of knowledge production, Orientalism, and Eurocentrism. Feminist scholars and activists, not only in the global south but also in Western contexts, have increasingly been at the forefront of criticising hegemonic notions of knowledge and have provided alternatives based on the social and oral histories and experiences of women and marginalised men. Many feminists have directly engaged with the intersections of capitalism and patriarchy.

Moreover, feminist scholars and activists have challenged the idea of universal sisterhood and essentialist notions of women as peace-makers, recognising that depending on class, ethnicity, race, religion etc. women can be complicit and directly involved in the marginalisation and oppression of other women and men. Women can also be perpetrators of violence. However, even if the concept of *jineoloji* might not reflect the rich and diverse histories of feminist thought and activism, it clearly plays an important role in the actual political struggle of Kurdish women activists who employ it strategically, as a form of knowledge production in a context where conservative and patriarchal norms are still prevailing.

Finally, a sympathetic critical engagement might also involve the question of leadership. If we take Öcalan's logic seriously and engage in the dismantling of state authority and hierarchical structures, we should also challenge the idea of the political leadership. We might want to ask questions about the place of critique within a truly democratic egalitarian and consensus-oriented society. When will it be possible to openly engage in constructive criticism of some of Öcalan's ideas without being side-lined as someone who just does not understand, is not revolutionary enough, or even worse considered a traitor? At which point can there be a diversification of sources and texts that shape some of the main principles of the movement? These questions are important, but can only really be asked and engaged with once Öcalan has gained his freedom. And these questions are not so much related to Öcalan himself, but to the political movement that is trying to implement and engage with his ideas. Yet, as long as he is imprisoned, it is only natural that his role is symbolic and exceeding that of a political leader who engages in the everyday negotiations of power and politics and who might be challenged. I very much hope that the day will come soon when Öcalan will be challenged by young Kurdish men and women, who all come together freely and in the spirit of peaceful democratic discussion and negotiation.

While one might not agree with every single idea and statement in Öcalan's writings, and while one might detect tensions, contraditions and problems within the Kurdish political movement, it should become obvious to the reader of this book that there is something incredibly refreshing, inspiring, constructive and positive in Öcalan's ideas and proposals. Much of what he says just makes lots of sense. Sadly, sense-making, rationality and evidence-based thinking appear to be losing ground at this historical juncture. I hope that the publication of this book will increase the number of people engaging with these important ideas that address many of the big questions of our time.

Introduction

On 20 March 1993, an illustrious group of Kurdish party leaders came together in Bar Elias, Lebanon for an unusual occasion. The Kurdistan Workers' Party (PKK) was declaring its first ever unilateral ceasefire.

The party had been founded in 1978 and saw no other way to wage the struggle for the rights of the Kurdish people than through an armed struggle, especially after the 1980 military coup in Turkey. Thus, the PKK took up arms in 1984, six years after it was founded and four years after the coup.

Eight and a half years later, the PKK's Abdullah Öcalan surprised friend and foe alike with the announcement that they were ready for a political solution within the existing borders of Turkey. This was probably the first time that Öcalan demonstrated – in front of Turkish TV cameras – that he was able to thwart expectations and develop new ideas. Widely regarded as a national liberation movement, the PKK never wanted to be merely a dogmatic copy of some organisational model along the lines laid out by some classical socialist author. The PKK was a movement in search of solutions, and at the heart of this search was Abdullah Öcalan.

Many people – again, friend and foe – did not take Öcalan's announcement seriously. They wanted to pigeonhole him as just another nationalist guerrilla leader and dismiss his offer as mere tactics. The ceasefire collapsed soon after the dubious death of Turgut Özal, the then President of Turkey, who had sent some positive signals for the resolution of the Kurdish question. But inside the Kurdish movement the search was on for new concepts.

Although the PKK was formed with a Marxist ideology and based on the Leninist party model, they had been very critical of the existing real-socialist models like the Soviet Union or Eastern Europe. This was especially the case in relation to the party model, bureaucracy, dictatorship of the proletariat and women's freedom. By 1991, the Soviet Bloc had all but collapsed and the same fate awaited many movements that defined themselves as socialist.

Since that day in Bar Elias, there have been many revolutionary changes to the paradigm of the PKK, sprouting especially from the discussions in the people's academy near Damascus. These discussions took place between Abdullah Öcalan and many revolutionaries and ordinary people alike, from 1993 to the day in autumn 1998 when he was forced out of Syria by the pressure applied not only by Turkey, but also by the USA. Based on his speeches and discussions in this school, philosophical and political analyses on different issues were published. Before Öcalan's abduction and incarceration in 1999, several books based upon his speeches on sex and gender were also published, among them three volumes of *Nasıl yaşamalı?* ('How to live?'), published from 1995 onwards. The title of a book of interviews with him, *Erkeği öldürmek* ('To kill the male'), became a well-known saying among Kurds.

Öcalan coined several slogans, such as 'A country can't be free unless the women are free', and later he restated this more strongly as 'To me women's freedom is more precious than the freedom of the homeland', thereby redefining national liberation as first and foremost women's freedom. In his prison writings, women's freedom is taken up constantly as an essential part of his discussions of history, contemporary society and political activism. The practice he observed in real socialist countries and his own theoretical efforts and practice since the 1970s led Öcalan to the conclusion that the enslavement of women was the origin of all other forms of enslavement. This, he concludes, is not due to woman being biologically different to man, but because she was the founder and leader of the Neolithic matriarchal system.

On 2 February 1999 a Falcon Jet landed at Jomo Kenyatta International Airport in Nairobi, Kenya. On board was Abdullah Öcalan, coming from Greece and expecting a short stopover on his way to South Africa where the Mandela government had agreed to grant him refuge. It is yet to be understood why the then Greek government chose Nairobi for Öcalan, especially since it was only months after a terrorist attack on the American Embassies in Nairobi and Dar es Salaam. The city was full of CIA and Mossad agents. Öcalan's journey through three continents and between cities such as Damascus, Athens, Moscow and Rome that had lasted for weeks was about to come to an end.

On 14 February 1999 another Falcon jet arrived at Wilson Airport, Nairobi. The pilot indicated he had come to pick up a group of businessmen. However, this was the jet which would 'render' the PKK leader to Turkey the next day. With the collaboration of the Kenyan authorities Öcalan was kidnapped and handed over to the Turkish military in an act of international piracy involving the CIA, the MIT (Turkish secret service), and Mossad. It was also supported by the governments of Russia, Greece and other European countries.

Thus ended a story of intrigue, deceit and an odyssey – fit for the movie screens – of Abdullah Öcalan and the Kurdish people. At the same time this was – and this is frequently ignored – a starting point not only for the CIA programme of secret abductions and renditions two and a half years prior to 9/11, but also for a new string of interventions into the Middle East which have brought our world to the brink of World War III. Öcalan's abduction and rendition remains a stain on the diplomatic history of all countries involved.

Earlier, in October 1998, Öcalan had come to Europe to seek support for a peaceful solution of the long lasting and bloody Turkish–Kurdish conflict. His hand held out for peace was refused. No country was willing to take the Kurdish leader, or to take the initiative in mediating negotiations between the conflicting parties. However, the die had already been cast and the Kurds were seen to be standing in the way of the geostrategic and economic interests of the leading powers in the Middle East. Deliberately, in order to gain political profit, these powers accepted the escalation of the war in Turkey. Abdullah Öcalan's abduction was supposed to be only the beginning.

For almost eleven years, from 1999 to 2009, Abdullah Öcalan was the sole prisoner on the prison island Imrali in the Turkish Marmara

Sea. Imrali prison is the unexposed Guantanamo of Europe. It is declared a military zone and guarded by 1,000 soldiers. Over the 18 years of Öcalan's imprisonment Imrali has had an arbitrary and continuous aggravated isolation regime in place. Bringing in a few other prisoners in 2009 has not altered this – on the contrary: the number of persons subjected to an aggravated isolation regime has increased. This regime was only relaxed slightly while a political process was in place; when there is no such process the regime becomes one of total isolation with no news from prisoners, no lawyer-client consultations, family visits, letters or telephone calls for any prisoner in Imrali (Öcalan has always been denied the right to phone).

Since July 2011 Öcalan has not seen his lawyers, since October 2014 his custodian and family have been barred from the island, and since April 2015 the political delegation of HDP parliamentarians could not confer with him after Turkish President Erdoğan halted talks with Öcalan and the PKK. The same restrictions applied also to the island's five other inmates. Since April 2014 we have had no independent information whatsoever from Imrali.

Although the anti-torture committee of the Council of Europe (CPT) has repeatedly sent a delegation to Imrali and demanded an end to his solitary confinement and the European Court of Human Rights delivered judgements regarding isolation, unfair trial and other issues, Turkey has not followed the recommendations or implemented the judgements. The Council of Europe's Committee of Ministers, its Parliamentary Assembly and even the Court itself have turned a blind eye to Turkey's human rights violations when it comes to Öcalan, and thus have become Turkey's accomplices.

The current total isolation of the whole Imrali Island Prison – which is now spilling over to other prisons – is not only unprecedented in the history of Turkey and a grave violation of the European Convention on Human Rights (ECHR). It is also an indication of the conflict's current and future escalation.

Öcalan inhabits a cell of 13 square meters. The construction of the cell and the airing grounds are such that he can see nothing but walls and sky – and even that only through a metal mesh. His books were written under extraordinary conditions. At times, he was isolated completely from the outside world, alone at the island prison for months. At others he was denied a pen and paper, or was not allowed to have more than one book in his possession at any one time. All 13 books that he penned in prison between 1999 and 2010 were handwritten. He never saw the manuscripts again, nor was he able to see them printed as books. He was also not able to discuss his thoughts with others as he put them down on paper. Despite such continuous harsh solitary confinement, the responsibility he felt for the resolution of the Kurdish issue led Öcalan to come up with profound solutions to many deep and complex issues and conflicts that face the Kurds – and ultimately everybody.

Öcalan has examined the issue of women's freedom, the phenomena of power and state and how interrelated they all are. This has led him over and over again to return to an analysis of history. In doing so he stumbled over nation, state and nation-state and how detrimental these are for any movement; turning even the most revolutionary individuals into mere practitioners of capitalism. For Abdullah Öcalan it is not sufficient to produce critique and self-critique. He feels compelled to lay out what might constitute an alternative to the way of life that is being imposed on society. Therefore, he makes an effort to systematise the lives and struggles of all those oppressed and exploited throughout history, as well as to propose an alternative model and way of life outside of capitalist modernity and thus classical civilisation.

These texts become ever more important in the light of developments in the region as well as in Kurdistan. At a time when war on women has been heightened around the world, his analysis exposes how the state truly represents the apex of such masculinity. The state is the institutionalisation of the hegemonic and dominant male. In addition, and as a natural result of this, the revival of sectarian and nationalist conflict in many areas of the world and the consequences of an aggressive capitalism confronting the world, Öcalan's proposals and an evident effort to implement them in

Rojava (Syrian Kurdistan) and Bakur (Turkish Kurdistan) might be just the right remedy for the war-stricken region. He calls upon all people to build and defend free life and humanity.

Thus, as you will see, Abdullah Öcalan interprets the right to self-determination of peoples not as the right to found a state, but aims rather for a stateless democracy; a non-state self-governance that he calls democratic confederalism and a democratic nation where the nation is not defined in relation to a state or an ethnic group.

The discussions on nation-state, women, intellectuals, religion and many such issues are not something new to the Kurdish people. What is new is the very clear rupture from all kinds of patriarchal mindsets. It was only after his abduction and the subsequent show trial in 1999 that his writings were published in Western languages. Thus, the misconception arose that these published writings constituted a complete turnaround in Öcalan's ideas. One thing that did change of course was the means of communication. His last public speech, his defence speech, at the courtroom in Imrali in 1999 was heavily censored by the Turkish authorities and reached the public only in printed form. From that point on, books became his most important medium of communication. He read hundreds of books and wrote more than a dozen.

In the 1999 show trial on Imrali Island, the Ankara State Security Court found Öcalan guilty of attempting to overthrow the constitutional order and sentenced him to death. Because of increasing international pressure and the resilience of Kurdish people's resistance the sentence was not carried out. In 2002 the death penalty was abolished in Turkey. Instead, a new law tailored for Öcalan was put into force: aggravated life sentence – prison until death with no possibility of parole. Öcalan lodged several complaints at the European Court of Human Rights in Strasbourg. The books he wrote are technically submissions to various courts, in Turkish called *savunmalar*, 'the defences', but are also a discussion of the Kurdish issue. Öcalan criticises the individual complaint mechanism at the European Court for Human Rights to which most of these submissions were addressed with the argument that his case is not an individual one. The uprising he initiated was the result of the ongoing suppression of the Kurdish people in Turkey. Likewise, the human rights violations he is facing in prison are not measures against an individual but against him as a symbol of the struggle for freedom. Therefore, his 'defences' – one is even called 'In Defence of a People' – are not individual defences but historical, political and philosophical writings dedicated to uncovering the roots of current conflicts and discussing solutions. The ever-deeper search for answers leads Öcalan back into a past before the establishment of patriarchy, class and state.

Shortly after Öcalan's abduction and rendition the International Initiative 'Freedom for Abdullah Öcalan – Peace in Kurdistan' was founded. It participated in and led many campaigns including the worldwide signature campaign 'Freedom for Abdullah Öcalan and the political prisoners in Turkey' which collected more than ten million signatures. Publishing Öcalan's writings has been an important function of the Initiative for many years. We strive not only to publish his works in different languages but also to prepare brochures compiled from his different books and focusing on specific topics. These brochures bring together the chain of his arguments on a specific topic which are otherwise spread over several books. This is necessary also because some of his works are still untranslated.

Four such brochures – collected here in newly edited versions as the chapters of this book – were compiled from the vast body of Öcalan's prison writings at different times. The first was called *War and Peace in Kurdistan* and was first published in 2008. At the time most of his works were still not translated into English or were unpublished. Knowing that the discussions in the Kurdish freedom movement had moved beyond the classical national liberation approach (the PKK, for instance, had deleted the aim of a separate state from their programme already in 1995), we realised that most of this was unknown to the general public. Therefore, we felt the need to clarify the current paradigm of the movement in the words of its most important thinker. A short description of the Kurdish question and a short history of the conflict was brought together with the background to the formation of the PKK and the transformation process that it went through.

Democratic Confederalism (2011) was meant to explain the concept of the same name that was first outlined in Öcalan's message at Newroz 2005. This was significant because many felt that interpreting the right to self-determination of peoples in a form other than the right to found a state seemed like settling for much less. They tended to link this shift to Öcalan's imprisonment at the hands of the Turkish state. We tried to show with this brochure that, on the contrary, democratic confederalism was an ambitious concept that requires a severe rupture from patriarchy.

That brochure was followed by *Liberating Life: Woman's Revolution* (2013), which presented Öcalan's view of history from the perspective of the freedom-loss of women. And he declared woman's revolution to be the liberation of all life – not only that of women. This resonated much in his coupling of *jin, jiyan, azadi* – that is woman, life, freedom.

Democratic Nation (2016) formulates a new definition of a nation; one that does not deny ethnicities and different cultures and is not coupled with a state. Such an approach to a nation is a remedy to the extremely politicised definitions of identities that are used by power monopolies to re-establish their own hegemony in backward ways.

These pages surely are not a complete framework for Öcalan's critique of the central civilisation nor his proposals for building a pro-women, pro-society and pro-individual philosophical and political way of life. His take on history, past revolutions and religion is similarly important and original. We hope to prepare them as brochures in the near future; alternatively, his books have been translated in full and these ideas can be chased through the books. We say chased, because there are many flows of thought that run in parallel and they are not ordinary – to say the least.

Abdullah Öcalan is not only a theorist; he is the leader of a movement that strives not only for the liberation of Kurdish people, but also to find answers to the question of how to live meaningfully.

This is why his writings have such impact on the lives of so many. He has been concerned with the issue of women's freedom all his life, and especially so during the struggle. He strongly encouraged women in the movement to take up the struggle against male dominance, providing inspiration through his critique of patriarchy. This approach and conduct from such an influential leader contributed to major political and social developments. For many years he spoke not only of the importance of surpassing constructed roles for women and men; he also encouraged the establishment of women's movements and institutions so that women can question and reshape themselves, their lives, men and society. Thus, hand in hand with the Kurdish liberation struggle, there has arisen in Kurdistan an unusually strong participation of women in all areas of life. In fact, the outstanding dynamism and vitality of the women's movement in Kurdistan often surprise the observer who does not expect this in a region of the world that is regarded as rather patriarchal.

Women's participation has achieved a lot of attention in the Rojava Revolution in Northern Syria. This revolution's main inspiration is Öcalan's writings. He continuously encourages everyone to take up intellectual work and to this end question and discuss everything – including his writings. These writings are intensively studied and heavily discussed by the Kurdish rebels and activists, and practical concepts are derived from these discussions. Therefore, what we have is an extraordinary connection between theory and praxis on a scale that is rarely to be found anywhere else in the world today.

Now in 2017, 18 years after Öcalan's abduction, Kurdish people stand at a totally different position; not only were they able to change their fate of being buried under the rubble, they are an active force in determining a rupture from all kinds of patriarchal regimes including capitalist modernity.

Öcalan's voice is tremendously important as one of peace and reason, but it is all too often silenced by his solitary confinement on Imrali Island. His freedom is in the interest of all peoples in the Middle East – not only of the Kurds. As you will see, the writings in this book do not address only the Kurds. There is no ethno-centrist or even nationalist perspective here. Everybody can be inspired by them or benefit from them. The Rojava Revolution may be the initial spark to a wave of transformations in the Middle East and perhaps beyond. And with the support of you, the reader, this wave will also carry Abdullah Öcalan himself out of his prison cell and to freedom.

Let us emphasise yet again; the texts included in this book should be regarded only as an incomplete framework and cannot replace the perusal of the full volumes of his writings. So please, don't content yourself with these compilations; our hope is that they will inspire you to immerse yourself in his books – from which these chapters are drawn.

International Initiative 'Freedom for
Abdullah Öcalan – Peace in Kurdistan'

I

War and Peace in Kurdistan: Perspectives on a Political Solution to the Kurdish Question

INTRODUCTION

Everyday life in the Middle East is dominated by numerous conflicts, which often appear strange to Western eyes as they seem to elude the Western understanding of reason and meaning. This is also true for the Kurdish question, one of the most complex and bloody fields of conflict in the Middle East still awaiting a solution. However, as long as we refrain from discussing all the dimensions of this conflict equally, it will continue and even be aggravated further, thus creating new and far-reaching problems. The historical, economic and political dimensions of the Kurdish question exceed by far the Arab-Israeli conflict, which, in contrast to the Kurdish question, enjoys the attention of the international public. Knowledge about this conflict is limited, and because it is taking place in one of the most central regions of the Middle East, both with respect to demography and to geostrategic importance, this deficit often results in one-sided and superficial analysis of this complex problem.

Since the settlement area of the Kurds spans the present territories of Arabs, Persians and Turks, the Kurdish question necessarily concerns most of the region. A solution in one part of Kurdistan also affects other parts of Kurdistan and neighbouring countries. Conversely, the destructive approach of actors in one country may have negative effects on potential solutions to the Kurdish question in other countries. The rugged Kurdish landscape is practically made for armed struggle, and the Kurds have been fighting colonisation or conquest by foreign powers since time immemorial. Resistance has become part of their life and culture.

At the beginning of every solution process the conflict needs to be recognised and defined. With a view to the Kurdish question, a realistic definition of the Kurdish *phenomenon* is therefore important. However, it is here that much of the disagreement begins. While the Arabs call the Kurds 'Arabs from Yemen', the Turks call them 'mountain Turks' and the Persians regard them as their ethnic counterparts. It is not astonishing, therefore, that their political stances on the Kurdish question are marked by arguments over definitions.

The Kurdish question has not been created out of the blue. It is the product of a long historical process and does not have much in common with similar issues in other parts of the world. In fact, there are a number of fundamental peculiarities and differences. Both of them need to be defined in a solution process. Any policy building merely on apparent common ground leads to irresolvable problems. A policy aiming at a solution needs to analyse realistically the phenomenon and include both the national, political and social background, and also all parties involved in the conflict. It is indispensable, therefore, to recognise the existence of the Kurdish phenomenon. This, however, is not possible without information about the historical background.

ETYMOLOGY OF THE WORDS
KURD AND *KURDISTAN*

The name Kurdistan goes back to the Sumerian word *kur*, which more than 5,000 years ago meant something like 'mountain'. The suffix *ti* stood for affiliation. The word *kurti* then had the meaning of *mountain tribe* or *mountain people*. The Luwians, who settled in western Anatolia about 3,000 years ago, called Kurdistan *Gondwana*, which in their language meant *land of the villages*. In Kurdish, *gond* is still the word for village. During the reign of Assure (from the early to mid Bronze Age through to the late Iron Age) the Kurds were called *Nairi*, which translates as 'people by the river'.

In the Middle Ages, under the reign of the Arab sultanates the Kurdish areas were referred to as *beled ekrad*. The Seljuk sultans who spoke Persian were the first to use the word *Kurdistan*, land of the Kurds, in their official communiqués. The Ottoman sultans also called the area settled by the Kurds Kurdistan. Until the 1920s, this name was generally used. After 1925 the existence of the Kurds was denied, particularly in Turkey.

KURDISH SETTLEMENT AREA
AND KURDISH LANGUAGE

They do exist, though. Kurdistan comprises an area of 450,000 square kilometres, which is surrounded by the settlement areas of the Persians, Azeris, Arabs and Anatolian Turks. It is one of the most mountainous, forested and water-rich areas in the Middle East and is pervaded by numerous fertile plains. Agriculture has been practised here for thousands of years. It was here that the Neolithic revolution began, when hunter-gatherers settled down and began farming the fields. The region is also called the *cradle of civilisation*. Thanks to its geographical position the Kurds have been able to protect their existence as an ethnic community until today. On the other hand, it was the exposed position of the Kurdish settlement area which often whetted the appetite of external powers and enticed them to embark on raids and conquest. The Kurdish language reflects the influence of the Neolithic revolution, which is believed to have begun in the region of the Zagros and Taurus mountains. Kurdish belongs to the Indo-European family of languages.

A SHORT OUTLINE OF KURDISH HISTORY

It is highly probable that Kurdish language and culture began to develop during the fourth ice age (20,000–15,000 BC). The Kurds are one of the oldest indigenous populations in the Middle Eastern region. About 6,000 BC they became distinct from other cultures. Historiography first mentions the Kurds as an ethnic group related to the *Hurrians* (3,000–2,000 BC). So it is assumed that the predecessors of the Kurds, the Hurrians and the descendants of the Hurrians – the *Mittani*, the *Nairi*, the *Urarteans* and the *Medes* – all lived in tribal confederations and kingdoms at the time. Kurdish society at the time was transitioning towards hierarchy and state structures, and can be seen as developing a strong patriarchy. Because during the Neolithic agricultural era women undertook more important functions within society, this led to women having more prominence within Kurdish society. It is highly likely that women relied on such strength for a long time and that this strength was drawn from the agricultural revolution.

It was Zoroastrianism which had a lasting impact on the Kurdish way of thinking, between 700 and 550 BC. Zoroastrianism cultivated a way of life that was marked by work in the fields, where men and women were equal to each other. Love of animals played an important role, and freedom was a high moral good. Zoroastrian culture influenced Eastern and Western civilisation equally, since both Persians and Hellenes adopted many of its cultural influences. The Persian civilisation, however, was founded by the Medes, believed to be the predecessors of the Kurds. In Herodotus' histories there is much evidence for a division of power among both Medes and Persian ethnic groups in the Persian Empire. This is also true for the subsequent Sassanid Empire.

The Hellenic era of classic antiquity left deep traces in the eastern hemisphere. The principalities Abgar in Urfa and Komagene, the centre of which was near Adiyaman-Samsat, and the kingdom of Palmyra in Syria were deeply influenced by the Greeks. One might say that it is there that we can find the first synthesis of oriental and occidental cultural influences. This special cultural encounter lasted until Palmyra was conquered by the Roman Empire in 269 AD, which brought about long-term negative consequences for the development of the entire region. The appearance of the Sassanid Empire did not end the Kurdish influence either. We may assume that during this time (216–652 AD) feudal structures were formed in Kurdistan. The development of feudalism reflects the divergence within ethnic structures. Kurdish society developed bonds of an increasingly feudal structure. At this developmental stage of feudalism the Islamic revolution occurred. Islam essentially transformed the strict relationships of slavery and ethnic bonds – which obstructed development – on the basis of urbanisation. At the same time a mental revolution regarding the ideological basis of feudal society began to develop.

The decline of the Sassanid Empire (650 AD) helped Islam create a feudal Kurdish aristocracy, which was strongly influenced by Arabisation. It became one of the strongest social and political formations of its time. The Kurdish dynasty of the *Ayyubids* (1175–1250 AD) evolved into one of the most potent dynasties in the Middle East, exercising great influence on the Kurds.

On the other hand, the Kurds maintained close relations to the Seljuk sultanate, which took over the rule from the Abbasids in 1055. Dynasties of Kurdish descent like the *Sheddadis, Buyidis* and *Marwanides* (990–1090) developed into feudal petty states. Other principalities followed. The ruling class of the Kurds enjoyed significant autonomy in the Ottoman Empire.

With the onset of the nineteenth century Kurdish history and society entered a new phase. In the course of deteriorating relations with the Ottomans several Kurdish uprisings occurred. English and French missionaries brought the idea of separatism into the Armenian and Aramaic churches, contributing to a chaotic situation. Furthermore, the relations between Armenians (Assyrians) and Kurds became notably worse. This fatal process ended in 1918 after World War I, with the almost complete physical and cultural annihilation of the Armenians and Aramaeans, who were the bearers of a culture several thousand years old.

Although the relations between Kurds and Turks had been seriously damaged, it did not result in a complete rupture like the Armenians and Arameans. This allowed for the continued physical existence of the Kurds.

STRUGGLES FOR RESOURCES,
WAR AND STATE TERROR IN KURDISTAN

In the past, its geostrategic position has made the country a pawn in struggles over the distribution of resources, and invited wars and state terror. This is still true today, and dates back into early history, as Kurdistan has been exposed to attacks and raids by external powers for its entire history. The terror regimes of the Assyrian and Scythian Empires between 1000 and 1300 BC, and the campaign of conquest by Alexander the Great, are the best-known examples. The Arab conquest after the onset of Islam triggered the Islamisation process of Kurdistan. Much as Islam as a word evokes peace it is an effective Arabic national war ideology and was able to spread quickly in Kurdistan. Islam proceeded into the foothills of the Taurus and Zagros mountains. Tribes that put up resistance were exterminated. In 1000 AD Islam had reached its peak in Kurdistan. Then in the thirteenth and fourteenth centuries the Mongols invaded Kurdistan. Flight and displacement followed. After the battle of Chaldiran in 1514, which saw the Ottomans victorious, the natural eastern border of the empire was shifted further eastward. The treaty of Qasr-e Shirin officially established the Iranian and Turkish borders and concluded the partition of Kurdistan, which has continued into the present. Mesopotamia and the Kurds found themselves for the most part within the borders of the Ottoman Empire. Until 1800 a relative peace had prevailed between the Ottomans and the Kurdish principalities, which was based on the Sunni denomination of Islam that they had in common. Alevitic and Zoroastrian Kurds, however, were defiant and took to resistance in the mountains.

After 1800, until the decline of the Ottoman Empire, Kurdistan was shaken by numerous rebellions, which were usually bloodily crushed. After the end of the Ottoman Empire the Kurdish partition deepened even further, exacerbating the atmosphere of violence. The rising imperialist powers of Britain and France redrew the boundaries in the Middle East and left Kurdistan under the rule of the Turkish republic, the Iranian peacock throne, the Iraqi monarchy and the Syrian-French regime.

Influenced by the loss of a large part of its former territories, Turkey switched to a strict policy of assimilation in order to enforce the unity of the remaining parts of its former empire. All indications of the existence of a culture other than Turkish were to be exterminated. They even banned the use of the Kurdish language.

The aspiring Pahlavi dynasty in Iran proceeded in the same way. The rebellion of the Kurdish tribal leader Simko Shikak from Urmiye and the emancipation struggle of the Kurdish republic of Mahabad were crushed in blood. The shah established a terror regime in the spirit of the nationalist-fascist epoch that rose at the beginning of the twentieth century. In the Iraqi and Syrian parts of Kurdistan, Britain and France suppressed the Kurdish emancipation efforts with the help of their Arab proxies. Here, too, a bloody colonial regime was established.

EUROPEAN COLONIALISM AND THE KURDISH DILEMMA

Driven by ambitions for geostrategic supremacy and boundless greed, the European intervention policy in the Middle East became increasingly colonialist at the beginning of the nineteenth century. Its primary goal became the submission and control of the Middle East. This added a new form of colonialisation to what the Kurds had already experienced over a history dating back into Sumerian times. However, Western capitalism changed it in unimagined ways. For the Kurds, this meant that they were again confronted with new colonialist actors and that the solution to the Kurdish question had become even more difficult.

With a view to their interests, the new imperialist powers deemed it more advantageous to seek cooperation with the sultan and the empire's administrative rulers in order to win allies, instead of breaking up the Ottoman Empire with unforeseeable consequences. This approach was meant to facilitate direct control over the region and to tame its rebellious peoples. This method, which was widespread throughout the British Empire, found its way into the history books as the 'divide and rule' strategy. In this way Ottoman rule was extended for another hundred years. France and Germany had similar strategies. The frictions between them did not influence the balance of power in the Middle East.

Yet another focus of imperial preservation of power was on the Christian ethnic groups. On the one hand, Western colonialism pretended to protect the Anatolian Greeks, Armenians and Aramaeans; on the other hand it incited them to rebel against the central power, which responded with repressive measures. The subsequent annihilation campaign was watched impassively by the Western powers. Eventually, this policy antagonised the nations of the Middle East. Again, the Kurds were only pawns in a game of foreign interests. In the past the Kurdish aristocracy had collaborated with the Arab and Turkish dynasties. Now they allowed foreign powers to use them as part of their colonialist intrigues. By winning the cooperation of the Kurds the British succeeded in tying the anxious Turkish and Arab rulers to their interests. Then again, they were able to further tie the Armenians and Aramaeans to the colonial powers, which in turn were hard-pressed by Kurdish feudal collaborators. However, the Turkish sultan, the Persian shah and the Arab rulers were not merely victims of this policy. They played a similar game in order to preserve their own power and to curb the greediness of the Western powers. It was the people who suffered.

THE IDEOLOGICAL BASIS OF COLONIAL OPPRESSION AND POWER POLITICS IN KURDISTAN

Both the partition of Kurdistan and ways in which the Arab, Persian and Turkish regimes ruled were social setbacks for the Kurds in each part of Kurdistan. The societal backwardness of today's Kurds, who still retain their feudal structures, is a product of these power relationships. With the coming of capitalist structures, from which the Kurds were mostly excluded, the development-related divide between them and the Arab, Turkish and Persian hegemonic societies grew larger. The power structures of feudal rule mingled with bourgeois-capitalist power structures, which helped to preserve the dominance of their corresponding nations. Although these structures depended on imperialism, they were able to build up their own national economies, further develop their own cultures, and stabilise their own state structures. In the areas of science and technology a national elite was coming of age. They forced all other ethnic groups in their countries to speak the official language. The media in the official language became a force on its own. With the help of a nationalist domestic and foreign policy they created a national ruling class, which saw itself as a hegemonic power with a view to other ethnic groups. The police and military were expanded and strengthened in order to break the resistance of the people. The Kurds were not able to respond to that. They were still suffering from the impacts of imperialism. They were confronted with an aggressive national chauvinism from the states that had power in Kurdistan, with the legitimacy of their power being explained through imaginative ideological constructions.

Denial and Self-Denial

The hegemonic powers (i.e. Turkey, Iraq, Iran and Syria) denied the Kurds their existence as an ethnic group. In such surroundings the Kurds ran a risk when they referred to their Kurdish roots. This is beyond being colonised. If people did so in spite of this, they could not even expect to be supported by members of their own ethnic group. For many Kurds, open commitment to their origin and culture resulted in exclusion from all economic and social relations. Therefore, many Kurds denied their ethnic descent or kept quiet about it – something that the respective regimes systematically encouraged. This denial strategy produced many absurdities. The chain of reasoning was that there was no such thing as the Kurds, if they did exist it was not very important, and if it was important it was dangerous to reveal them. For the Arab regime, they feel that the Islamic conquests give them the right. Can there be a greater right than to conquer in the name of God? This is the premise and is still strongly put forth.

The Persians went a step further and declared the Kurds to be an ethnic subgroup of the Persians. In this way, the Kurds were granted all their rights in a natural way. Kurds who nonetheless demanded their rights and stuck to their ethnic identity were regarded as people who threw mud at their own nation and who therefore received the appropriate treatment.

The Turkish regime derived its claim to supremacy over the Kurds from alleged campaigns of conquest in Anatolia a thousand years ago. There had not been other peoples there. Therefore, *Kurd* and *Kurdistan* are non-words, non-existent and not allowed to exist according to the official ideology. These words are unimportant and dangerous, and their use can even amount to an act of terrorism and is punished correspondingly.

Assimilation

Hegemonic powers often use assimilation as a tool when they are confronted with defiant ethnic groups. Language and culture are also carriers of potential resistance, which can be desiccated by assimilation. Banning the native language and enforcing the use of a foreign language are effective tools. People who are no longer able to speak their native language will no longer cherish its characteristics, which are rooted in ethnic, geographic and cultural factors. Without the unifying element of language the uniting quality of collective ideas also disappears. Without this common basis the collective ties within the ethnic group break up and become lost. Consequently, hegemonic language and culture gain ground in the conquered ethnic and language environment. Forced use of the hegemonic language results in a withering of the native language until it becomes irrelevant. This happens even faster when the native language is not a literary language, as is the case with Kurdish. An assimilation strategy is not restricted to the use of language – it is applied in all public and social areas controlled by the state.

Kurdistan has often been the stage of cultural assimilation attempts by foreign hegemonic powers. The last hundred years of its history, however, have been the most destructive. The creation of modern nation-state structures in the hegemonic countries, and the creation of a colonial system of rule in Kurdistan, aggravated the assimilation attempts directed at the Kurdish language and culture.

Like Persian and Arabic previously, now Turkish, too, became a hegemonic language by force. The Kurds of the past, before modernity had been able to preserve their culture and language, were now pushed back by three hegemonic languages and cultures, which also had modern media and communication tools at their disposal. Traditional Kurdish songs and literature were banned. Thus, the existence of the Kurdish language, which had produced many works of literature in the Middle Ages, was threatened. Kurdish culture and language were declared subversive elements. Native language education was banned. The hegemonic languages became the only languages that were allowed in the education system, and thus the only languages used to teach the achievements of modernity.

The Turkish, Persian and Arab nation-states pursued a systematic assimilation policy using varying repressive means – both institutionally and socially – denying Kurdish language and culture any legitimacy. Only the language and culture of the hegemons were supposed to survive.

Religion and Nationalism

The hegemonic powers also used religion and nationalism to preserve their supremacy. In all parts of Kurdistan, Islam is a state religion used as a tool for controlling the population. Even if these regimes embrace secularism, the entanglement of political and religious institutions is obvious. While in Iran there is an openly theocratic regime in power, in other countries the instrumentalisation of religion for political interests is kept concealed. In the

Turkish state religious authorities employ more than a hundred thousand Imams. Perhaps even Iran does not possess such an army of religious leaders. The religious schools are under the direct control of the state. Quran schools and theological institutes and faculties employ almost half a million people. This makes the constitutional postulate of secularism look absurd and rather like a varnish.

In addition, wherever sectarianism meets active politics it produces even more chaotic situations. Under the DP (Democracy Party) and the AP (Justice Party) governments, religion was openly politicised. The military coups in March 1971 and September 1980 modified the Turkish ideological framework and redefined the role of religion. This initiated a re-Islamisation of the Turkish republic, in a similar way to what had happened in Iran after Khomeini had seized power in 1979, albeit not as radical. In 2003 the AKP (Justice and Development Party) came into power and with it, for the first time, came Islamic ideologues. This election victory was no accident, but was the result of the long-term religious policy of the Turkish state.

Bourgeois Nationalism

Another ideological tool of the hegemonic powers is the nationalism of the bourgeoisie. This ideology was most important in the nineteenth and twentieth centuries, when it became the dominant ideology of the nation-states. It formed the basis for the bourgeoisie to proceed against the interests of the workers and real socialist[1] tendencies. Eventually, nationalism emerged as a logical result of the nation-state bearing almost religious features.

The Turkish form of nationalism that came into being after 1840 was an attempt to prevent the decay of the Ottoman Empire, which had begun to show. Early Turkish nationalists were originally legalists. Later they turned against the sultanate of Abdulhamid II and became increasingly radical. The nationalism of the Young Turk movement expressed itself in the Committee for Unity and

---

1   The term 'real socialist' refers to countries/systems that embodied 'really existing socialism' such as the USSR, China and Cuba.

Progress, which worked for constitutional reform of the state and aspired towards gaining power within the empire. Apart from that they had made it clear that they wanted to strengthen the empire again, which was externally weak and internally threatened by decay, by systematically modernising it politically, militarily and economically. The opening of Germany's foreign policy towards the Middle East and Central Asia then added a racist component to Turkish nationalism. The genocide of the Armenians, Pontic Greeks, Aramaeans and Kurds followed. The young Turkish republic was marked by aggressive nationalism and a very narrow understanding of the nation-state. The slogan 'one language, one nation, one country' became a political dogma. Although in principle this was a classless state approach that did not grant privileges, the instruments to actually implement it were lacking. Its abstractness carried the danger of ideological fanaticism. Nationalism degraded into a tool of the ruling circles and was used mostly to cover up their failures. Under the flag of the 'superior Turkish identity' the entire society was sworn to an aggressive nationalism.

The war in Kurdistan and the state terrorism this involved created a separate power block. As in other systems where certain power blocks derive their power from military potential and base their existence on war, so they formed the Turkish society accordingly.

This is also why the political system lost its ability to solve conflicts. This is a system that has been formed by war and state terror, where it remains unclear which power centres serve which interests and goals – with equally disastrous effects for Turkish and Kurdish communities.

KURDISH IDENTITY AND KURDISH RESISTANCE

The identification process of the Kurds as a nation occurred comparatively late. Even if there was a commitment to being Kurdish in the Kurdish rebellions of the nineteenth century, it did not go beyond opposition against the sultanate and the rule of the shah. There were no ideas regarding alternative forms of life. A commitment to the Kurdish identity involved the creation of a Kurdish kingdom, in the sense of the traditional sultanates. For a long time the Kurds were far from identifying themselves as a nation. It was only in the second half of the twentieth century that the idea of a Kurdish identity began to develop in the course of intellectual debates, mostly from the Turkish left. However, this shift lacked the intellectual potential to overcome more traditional ideas of Kurdish identity affiliated with tribal order and sheikdom. Both the real socialist-leaning communist parties and the liberal and feudal parties struggled to understand the idea of a Kurdish nation or the idea of the Kurds as an ethnic group. Only the left-leaning student movement of the 1970s was able to contribute substantially to the awareness that there was a Kurdish identity.

The ethnic identification process developed in the conflictual relationship between Turkish chauvinist nationalism and Kurdish feudal nationalism. On the one hand there was the confrontation with the ideological hegemony of the system, which was often dressed up to look left-wing, and on the other hand there was the confrontation with the Kurdish aristocracy, who traditionally cooperated with the system. Liberation from these societal, political and ideological forces did not come easy. It required both intellectual debate and practical organisational work. This led directly to resistance. The Kurdish emancipation efforts had not yet come of age in the 1970s, but after 35 years had passed Kurds had become more aware of their own identity and offered approaches for a solution of the Kurdish question. It is also true that the Kurds and their emancipation cannot be suppressed by force in the long term. No system can survive for long, when it tries to transform its social contradiction forcibly. The Kurdish emancipation efforts also demonstrate that people cannot develop if they do not reconquer their societal dignity.

THE KURDISTAN WORKERS PARTY (PKK)

Short Outline of the History of Origins of the PKK

In April 1973, a group of six people came together in order to form an independent Kurdish political organisation. They acted on the assumption that Kurdistan was a classic colony, where the population was forcibly refused their right to self-determination. It was their prime goal to change this. This gathering may also be called the birth of a new Kurdish movement.

Over the years, this group found new followers who helped them spread their beliefs within the rural population of Kurdistan. More and more they clashed with Turkish security forces, armed tribesmen of the Kurdish aristocracy and rival political groups, which violently attacked the young movement. On 27 November 1978, the Kurdistan Workers Party (PKK) was founded in a small village near Diyarbakir. Twenty-two leading members of the movement took part in the inaugural meeting in order to set up more professional structures for the movement. In an urban environment the movement would not have survived, so they focused their activities on the rural Kurdish regions.

The Turkish authorities reacted harshly to the propaganda efforts of the PKK. Detentions and armed clashes followed. Both sides experienced losses. The situation in Turkey, however, was also coming to a head. The first signs of an imminent military coup were already visible in 1979. The PKK responded by withdrawing into the mountains or into other Middle Eastern countries. Only a small number of activists remained in Turkey. This step helped the PKK to secure their survival. On 12 September 1980, the Turkish military overthrew the civil government and seized power. Many of the PKK cadres who had remained in Turkey were imprisoned by the military junta.

In this situation, the PKK had to determine whether they wanted to become an exile organisation or a modern national liberation movement. After a short phase of reorganisation, a majority of members returned to Kurdistan and took up armed resistance against the fascist junta. The attacks on military facilities in Eruh and Şemdinli on 15 August 1984, proclaimed the official beginning of the armed resistance. Although there were setbacks, the move towards becoming a national liberation movement had been made.

Originally the Turkish authorities – Turgut Ozal had just been elected prime minister – tried to play down the incident. State propaganda called the guerrillas a 'handful of bandits', which showed the mindset of those in charge. A political approach to the conflict was not conceivable. The clashes grew into a war, which claimed numerous victims from either side.

It was only in the 1990s that the situation became less gridlocked, when the state seemed to become ready for a political solution. There were statements by Turgut Ozal and Suleyman Demirel, then president, indicating that they might recognise the Kurdish identity, raising hopes for an early end of the conflict. The PKK tried to strengthen this process by declaring a ceasefire in 1993. The sudden death of Turgut Ozal deprived this process of one of its most important protagonists. There were other obstacles, too. Some hardliners among the PKK stuck to the armed struggle; the situation among the leadership of the Turkish state was difficult and marked by conflicting interests; the attitude of the Iraqi-Kurdish leaders Talabani and Barzani was also not helpful in furthering the peace process. Up to that point it was the biggest opportunity for a peaceful solution to the Kurdish question, and it was lost.

Subsequently the conflict escalated. Both parties experienced large losses. However, even this escalation did not lift the deadlock. The years of war between 1994 and 1998 were lost years. In spite of several unilateral ceasefires on the part of the PKK, the Turkish state insisted on a military solution – they didn't even respond to the PKK ceasefire in 1998. Rather, it stirred up a military confrontation between Turkey and Syria, which brought both countries to the edge of a war. In 1998 I went to Europe as the chairman of the PKK in order to promote a political solution. The following odyssey is well known. I was abducted from Kenya and brought to Turkey in violation of international law. This abduction was backed by an alliance of secret services from different countries, and the public expected the conflict to escalate further. However, the trial on the Turkish prison island of Imrali marked a political U-turn in the conflict, and offered new possibilities for a political solution.

At the same time, this turn caused the PKK to reorient itself ideologically and politically. I had been working on these issues before my abduction. This was truly an ideological and political break. But what, then, were the real motives?

Main Criticism

Doubtless my abduction was a heavy blow for the PKK. It was nonetheless not the reason for the ideological and political shift. The PKK had been conceived as a party with a state-like hierarchical structure similar to other parties. Such a structure, however, causes it to contradict dialectically the principles of democracy, freedom and equality: a contradiction in principle concerning all parties whatsoever their philosophy. Although the PKK stood for freedom-oriented views, we had not been able to free ourselves from thinking in hierarchical structures.

Another contradiction lay in the PKK's quest for institutional political power, which correspondingly formed and aligned the party. Structures aligned along the lines of institutional power, however, are in conflict with societal democratisation, which the PKK was espousing. Activists of any such party tend to orient themselves according to their superiors rather than society, or in a way that demonstrates their aspiration to such positions themselves. All of the three big ideological tendencies based on emancipative social conceptions have been confronted with this contradiction. Real socialism and social democracy, as well as national liberation movements when they tried to set up social conceptions beyond capitalism, could not free themselves from the ideological constraints of the capitalist system. Early on, they became pillars of the capitalist system while seeking institutional political power instead of focusing on the democratisation of society.

Another contradiction was the value of war in the ideological and political considerations of the PKK. War was understood as the continuation of politics by different means, and was romanticised as a strategic instrument.

This was a blatant contradiction of our self-perception as a movement struggling for the liberation of society. According to this, the use of armed force can only be justified for the purpose of necessary self-defence. Anything beyond that would be in violation of the socially emancipative approach that the PKK felt itself obliged to uphold, since repressive regimes throughout history have been based on war or have aligned their institutions according to the logic of warfare. The PKK believed that the armed struggle would be sufficient for winning the rights that the Kurds had been denied. Such a deterministic idea of war is neither socialist nor democratic, although the PKK saw itself as a democratic party. A really socialist party is neither oriented by state-like structures and hierarchies nor does it aspire to institutional political power, the basis of which is the protection of interests and power by war.

The supposed defeat of the PKK that the Turkish authorities believed they had accomplished through my abduction was eventually reason enough to look, critically and openly, into the reasons that had prevented us from making better progress with our liberation movement. The ideological and political change the PKK underwent turned an apparent defeat into a gateway to new horizons.

NEW STRATEGIC, PHILOSOPHICAL AND POLITICAL APPROACHES

A comprehensive treatment of the main strategic, ideological, philosophical and political elements underpinning the process of change cannot be accomplished in this chapter.

However, the cornerstones can be outlined as follows:

- The philosophical, political and value-related approaches that the newly aligned PKK embraces find adequate expression in what is called 'democratic socialism'.
- The PKK does not derive the creation of a Kurdish nation-state from the right of the people to self-determination. However,

we regard this right as the basis for the establishment of grassroots democracies, without seeking new political borders. It is up to the PKK to convince Kurdish society of their conviction. This is also true for any dialogue with hegemonic countries exercising power in Kurdistan. It is to be the basis for a solution of the existing issues.

- The countries that presently exist here need democratic reforms going beyond mere lip-service to democracy. It is not realistic, though, to go for the immediate abolition of the state. This does not mean that we have to take it as it is. The classic state structure with its despotic attitude towards power is unacceptable. The institutional state needs to be subjected to democratic changes. At the end of this process, there should be a lean state existing simply as a political institution, which only functions in the fields of internal and external security and in the provision of social security. Such an idea of the state has nothing in common with the authoritarian character of the classic state, but would rather be regarded as a general public authority.

- The Kurdish liberation movement is working for a system of democratic self-organisation in Kurdistan with the features of a confederation. Democratic confederalism is understood as a non-state democratic nation organisation. It provides a framework, within which *inter alia* minorities, religious communities, cultural groups, gender-specific groups and other societal groups can organise autonomously. This model may also be seen as a way of organising a democratic nation and culture. The democratisation process in Kurdistan is not limited to matters of form but, rather, proposes a broad societal project aiming at economic, social and political sovereignty in all parts of society. It advances the building of necessary institutions and creates the instruments for democratic self-government and control. It is a continuous and long-term process. Elections are not the only means in this context. Rather, this is a dynamic political process which needs direct intervention by the sovereign, the people. The people are to be directly involved in the institutionalisation, governance and supervision of their own economic, social and political formations. This project builds on the self-government of local communities and is organised in the form of open councils, town councils, local parliaments and larger congresses. The citizens themselves are the agents of this kind of self-government, not state-based authorities. The principle of federal self-government has no restrictions. It can even be continued across borders in order to create multinational democratic structures. Democratic confederalism prefers flat hierarchies so as to further discussions and decision-making at the level of communities.

- The model outlined here may also be described as people's democratic self-governance in Kurdistan plus the state as the general public authority, where the state-related sovereign rights are only limited. Such a model allows a more adequate implementation of basic values like freedom and equality than traditional administrative models. This model need not be restricted to Turkey, but may also be applicable in the other parts of Kurdistan. Simultaneously, this model is suitable for the building of federal administrative structures in all Kurdish settlement areas in Syria, Turkey, Iraq and Iran. Thus, it is possible to build confederate structures across all parts of Kurdistan without the need to question the existing borders.

- The decline of real socialism was also a result of how socialist countries used their power both internally and externally, and of the fact that they misconceived the importance of the gender issue. Women and power seem to be contradictory things. In real socialism, the question of women's rights was a subordinate issue which, it was believed, would be resolved once economic and other societal problems were solved. However, women may also be regarded as an oppressed class and nation or an oppressed gender. As long as we do not discuss freedom and equal treatment of women in a historical and societal context, as long as no adequate theory has been devised, there will not be an adequate practice either. Therefore, women's liberation must assume a key strategic role in the democratic struggle for freedom in Kurdistan.

- Today, the democratisation of politics is one of the most urgent challenges we face. However, democratic politics needs democratic parties. As long as there are no parties and party-affiliated institutions committed to the interests of the society instead of fulfilling state orders, a democratisation of politics will not be possible. In Turkey, parties are simply propaganda tools of the rentier state and are nothing but instruments that distribute rents once they are in power. Their transformation into parties committed exclusively to the interests of society, and the creation of the necessary legal basis to facilitate this, would be an important part of any political reform. The founding of parties bearing the word Kurdistan in their name is still a criminal act. Independent parties are still obstructed in many ways. Kurdistan-related parties in coalitions serve democratisation as long as they do not advocate separatism or the use of violence.

- There is a widespread individual and institutional subservient spirit, which is one of the biggest obstacles blocking democratisation. It can only be overcome by creating an awareness of democracy in all parts of society. Citizens must be invited actively to commit themselves to democracy. For the Kurds, this means building democratic structures in all parts of Kurdistan and wherever there are Kurdish communities, which advance the active participation in the political life of the community. Minorities living in Kurdistan must be invited to participate as well. The development of grassroots-level democratic structures and a corresponding practical approach must have top priority. Such grassroots structures must be regarded as obligatory, even where basic democratic and legal principles are violated as in the Middle East.

- Politics needs independent media. Without them state structures will not develop any sensitivity to questions of democracy. Nor will it be possible to bring democracy into politics. Freedom of information is not only a right of the individual. It also involves a societal dimension. Furthermore, independent media always have a societal mandate. Their communication with the public must be marked by democratic balance.
- Feudal institutions like tribes, sheikdom, aghas and sectarianism, which are essentially relics of the Middle Ages, are like the institutions of classic nation-states – obstacles preventing democratisation. They must be urged to join in with democratic change. These parasitic institutions must be overcome as a priority.
- The right to native language education must be respected. Even if the authorities do not advance such education, they must not impede civic efforts to create institutions offering Kurdish language and culture education. The health system must be legitimised by both state and civil society.
- An ecological model of society is essentially socialist. The establishment of an ecological balance will only be accomplished during the transition phase from an alienated class society based on despotism to a socialist society. It would be an illusion to hope for the conservation of the environment in a capitalist system. These systems largely participate in ecological devastation. Protection of the environment must be given broad consideration in the process of societal change.
- The solution to the Kurdish question will be realised within the framework of the democratisation of the countries exercising hegemonic power over different parts of Kurdistan. This process is not limited to these countries, but rather extends across the entire Middle East. The freedom of Kurdistan is tied to the democratisation of the Middle East. A free Kurdistan is only conceivable as a democratic Kurdistan.

- Individual freedom of expression and decision is indefeasible. No country, no state, no society has the right to restrict these freedoms, whatever reasons they may cite. Without the freedom of the individual there will be no freedom for society, just as freedom for the individual is impossible if society is not free.

- A just redistribution of the economic resources presently in the possession of the state is particularly important for the liberation of society. Economic supply must not become a tool in the hands of the state for exercising pressure on the people. Economic resources are not the property of the state but of society. An economy close to the people should be based on such redistribution and be use value-oriented instead of exclusively pursuing an economy based on commodification and profit. The profit-based economy has not only damaged society but also the environment. One of the main reasons for the decline of society lies in the level of expansion of financial markets. The artificial production of needs, the more and more adventurous search for new sales markets and the boundless greed for ever-growing profits lets the divide between rich and poor steadily grow and enlarges the army of those living below the poverty line or even dying of hunger. Humanity can no longer sustain itself with such an economic policy. This is therefore the biggest challenge for socialist politics: progressive transition from a commodity-oriented society to a society producing on the basis of use value; from production based on profit to production based on sharing.

- Although Kurds assign a high value to the family, this is still a place where freedom does not abound. Lack of financial resources, lack of education and lack of health care do not allow for much development. The situation for women and children is disastrous. So-called honour killings of female family members are a symbol of this disaster. They become the targets of an archaic notion of honour, which reflects the degeneration of the entire society. Male frustration over existing conditions is directed against the supposedly weakest members of the society: women. The family as a social institution experiences a crisis. Here, too, a solution can only be found in the context of an overall democratisation.

THE PRESENT SITUATION AND SUGGESTIONS FOR A SOLUTION

Kurdish–Turkish relations in Turkey play a key role with a view to a solution to the Kurdish question. The Kurds in Iran, Iraq and Syria alone can not bring about an overall solution to the Kurdish question. The Kurds in Iraq are a good example. The semi-state Kurdish autonomy is indirectly the result of worldwide efforts on the part of Turkey, the USA and their allies to denounce the PKK as a terror organisation. Without consent by Ankara this 'solution' would not have been possible. The chaos caused by this solution is obvious, and the result unforeseeable. It is also unclear which direction the feudal-liberal Kurdish national authority in Iraq will take in the long run and how it will affect Iran, Syria and Turkey. There is the danger of a regional escalation of the conflict similar in shape to the Israeli-Palestinian conflict. A flare-up of Kurdish nationalism might even radicalise the Persian, Arab and Turkish nationalists further, making a solution to the problem more difficult.

This prospect needs to be contrasted with a solution free of nationalist aspirations, which recognises existing territorial borders. In return, the status of the Kurds will be made official in each country's constitution, thus enshrining their rights concerning culture, language and political participation. Such a model would be largely in accordance with the historical and societal realities of the region.

In light of this, making peace with the Kurds seems inevitable. It is highly improbable that the present war or any future war will yield anything but a Pyrrhic victory. Therefore, this war must be ended. It has lasted too long already. It is in the interest of all countries in the region to follow the example of other countries and take the necessary steps.

The Kurds only demand that their existence be respected; they demand freedom of culture and a fully democratic system. A more humane and modest solution is impossible. The examples of South Africa, Wales, Northern Ireland, Scotland and Corsica demonstrate the ways in which different modern countries have been able to solve similar problems in the course of their history. Furthermore, these comparisons help us to find a more objective approach to our own problems.

Turning our backs on violence as a means of solving the Kurdish question, and overcoming the repressive policy of denial at least in part, are closely connected to the fact that we upheld the democratic option. The ban on Kurdish language and culture, education and broadcasting is in itself a terrorist act and practically invites counter-violence. Violence, however, has been used by both sides to an extent that goes beyond legitimate self-defence.

Many movements today take to even more extreme methods. However, we have declared unilateral ceasefires several times – we have withdrawn large numbers of our fighters from Turkish territory, and thus refuted the accusation of terrorism. Our peace efforts, however, have been ignored over the years. Our initiatives were never met with a response. Rather, a group of Kurdish politicians sent out as ambassadors of peace was detained and handed long prison terms.[2] Our efforts for peace have wrongly been interpreted

---

2 On 29 August 1998, Abdullah Öcalan declared a ceasefire that would start on 1 September 1998. In the weeks that immediately followed this announcement Öcalan was forced out of Syria, and after an odyssey of several months he was abducted from Kenya and handed over to the Turkish authorities. Öcalan continued his efforts for peace from the Imrali Island Prison that had been especially tailored for him, and where he was the sole prisoner. He declared a ceasefire on 2 August 1999, and called on PKK forces to withdraw outside the boundaries of the borders of Turkey. These forces were immediately withdrawn, but during the withdrawal many PKK guerrillas lost their lives because they were ambushed by Turkish army forces. In parallel, Öcalan asked for symbolic peace groups to come

as weakness. There is no other explanation for statements like 'the PKK and Öcalan are practically finished', or that our initiatives were only tactical. So they claimed they only needed to act a little bit tougher in order to smash the PKK. So they increased their attacks on the Kurdish liberation movement. Nobody asks, however, why they never succeeded. It is impossible to solve the Kurdish question by means of violence. The attitude described above also contributed to the failure of the ceasefire that began on 1 October 2006. I had called on the PKK to offer this ceasefire. Some intellectuals and non-government organisations had demanded such a step. However, again it was not taken seriously. Instead, racism and chauvinism were stirred up, creating an atmosphere of confrontation. Besides, we must not forget that the AKP also uses this issue to play down their own problems with the Kemalist elite, by making compromises with the army and speculating on the escalation of the Kurdish problem. Presently, the government restricts itself to some half-hearted measures in order to wrench some concessions from the EU. They are trying to win time with the help of the harmonisation laws enacted in the context of the EU accession process. In reality, these supposed reforms are just waste-paper.

The exacerbating conflict is cause for concern. Nevertheless, I will not give up my hopes for a just peace. It can become possible at any time.

I offer Turkish society a simple solution. We demand a democratic nation. We are not opposed to the unitary state and republic. We accept the republic, its unitary structure and laicism. However, we believe that it must be redefined as a democratic state that respects peoples, cultures and rights. On this basis, the Kurds must be free to organise in a way that revitalises their culture and language and allows them to develop economically and ecologically. This would allow Kurds, Turks and other cultures to come together under the

---

to Turkey as an indication of good will. As a result, on 1 October 1999 the first peace group consisting of eight people came from Qandil, and on 29 October 1999 a second peace group also consisting of eight people came from Europe.

roof of a democratic nation in Turkey. This is only possible, though, with a democratic constitution and an advanced legal framework warranting respect for different cultures.

Our idea of a democratic nation is not defined by flags and borders. Our idea of a democratic nation embraces a model based on democracy instead of a model based on state structures and ethnic origins. Turkey needs to define itself as a country which includes all ethnic groups. This would be a model based on human rights instead of religion or race. Our idea of a democratic nation embraces all ethnic groups and cultures.

Against this background, let me summarise the solution I propose:

- The Kurdish question is to be treated as a fundamental question of democratisation. The Kurdish identity must be put down in the constitution and integrated in the legal system. The new constitution shall contain an article with the following wording: 'The constitution of the Turkish republic recognises the existence and the expression of all its cultures in a democratic way.' This would be sufficient.
- Cultural and language rights must be protected by law. There must not be any restrictions on radio, TV or the press. Kurdish programmes and programmes in other languages must be treated by the same rules and regulations as Turkish programmes. The same must be true for cultural activities.
- Kurdish should be taught in elementary schools. People who want their children to get such an education must be able to send them to such a school. High schools should offer lessons on Kurdish culture, language and literature as elective courses. Universities must be permitted to establish institutes for Kurdish language, literature, culture and history.
- The freedom of expression and organisation must not be restricted. Political activities must not be restricted or regulated by the state. This must also be true in the context of the Kurdish question without restriction.

- Party and election laws must be subjected to democratic reform. The laws must allow the participation of the Kurdish people and all other democratic groups in the process of democratic decision-making.
- The village-guard system and the illegal networks[3] within state structures must be disbanded.
- People who were evicted from their villages during the war must be allowed to return without impediment. All administrative, legal, economic or social measures necessary must be met. Furthermore, a developmental programme must be initiated in order to help the Kurdish population to earn a living and improve their standard of living.
- A law for peace and participation in the society should be enacted. This law would enable the members of the guerrilla movement, the imprisoned and those who are in exile to take part in public life without any preconditions.

Additionally, immediate measures regarding how to reach a solution need to be discussed. A democratic action plan must be formulated and put into practice. In order to reconcile society, truth and justice commissions need to be set up. Both sides must find out what they have done wrong and discuss it openly. This is the only way to achieve the reconciliation of society.

Whenever states or organisations cannot make progress anymore, intellectuals may serve as mediators. South Africa, Northern Ireland and Sierra Leone have had positive experiences with this model. They may take the role of arbitrators, with whose help both parties can be moved in the direction of a just peace. The commissions may include intellectuals, lawyers, physicians or scientists. When the day

---

3   Village guards are paramilitaries that are mostly recruited from the Kurdish population. They are set up and funded by the Turkish state to fight against the PKK and they are involved in the extrajudicial killing, torture and disappearance of people. The illegal networks include organisations such as Jandarma İstihbarat ve Terörle Mücadele (JİTEM) or Jandarma İstihbarat Teşkilatı (JİT) and Ergenekon.

comes that we put down our arms, it will only be into the hands of such a commission, provided it is a commission that is determined to achieve justice.

Why would we surrender our arms without the prospect of justice? The beginning of such a process also depends on goodwill and dialogue. Should a dialogue come about, we will be able to begin a process similar to the last unlimited ceasefire.

I am prepared to do all I can. The government, however, needs to show its desire for peace. It needs to take the initiative. This is what they need to do if they do not wish to be solely responsible for the consequences.

If our efforts for a peaceful solution fail, or are sacrificed in the name of day-by-day politics, power struggles or profit-seeking, the present conflict will exacerbate and its end will be unpredictable. The chaos following will see no winners.

At last, Turkey needs to muster the strength to recognise its own reality, the reality of Kurdish existence and global dynamics. A state which denies reality will eventually and inevitably find itself on the brink of existence.

It is crucial, therefore, to take the steps that will lead this country to a lasting peace.

2

Democratic Confederalism

INTRODUCTION

For more than 30 years the Kurdistan Workers' Party (PKK) has been struggling for the legitimate rights of the Kurdish people. Our struggle, our fight for liberation turned the Kurdish question into an international issue which affected the entire Middle East and brought a solution to the Kurdish question within reach.

When the PKK was formed in the 1970s the international ideological and political climate was characterised by the bipolar world of the Cold War and the conflict between the socialist and the capitalist camps. The PKK was inspired at that time by the rise of decolonialisation movements all over the world. In this context we tried to find our own way in agreement with the particular situation in our homeland. The PKK never regarded the Kurdish question as a mere problem of ethnicity or nationhood. Rather, we believed, it was a question of democracy and revolution. These aims have increasingly determined our actions since the 1990s.

We also recognised a causal link between the Kurdish question and the global domination of the modern capitalist system. Without questioning and challenging this link a solution would not be possible. Otherwise we would only become involved in new dependencies.

With a view to issues of ethnicity and nationhood like the Kurdish question, which have their roots deep in history and at the foundations of society, there seemed to be only one viable solution: the creation of a nation-state, which was the paradigm of the capitalist modernity at that time.

We did not believe, however, that any ready-made political blueprints would be able to improve the situation of the people in the Middle East in a way that was sustainable. Had it not been nationalism and nation-states that had created so many of the problems in the Middle East?

Let us therefore take a closer look at the historical background of this paradigm and see whether we can map a solution that avoids the trap of nationalism and fits the situation of the Middle East better.

THE NATION-STATE

Basics

With the sedentarisation of people they began to form an idea of the area that they lived in, its extension and its boundaries, which were mostly determined by nature and the features of the landscape. Clans and tribes that had settled in a certain area and lived there for a long period of time developed the notions of a common identity and of a homeland. The boundaries between what the tribes saw as their homelands were not yet borders. Commerce, culture or language were not restricted by boundaries. Territorial borders remained flexible for a long time. Feudal structures prevailed almost everywhere, and now and then dynastic monarchies or great multi-ethnic empires rose with continuously changing borders and many different languages and religious communities, such as the Roman Empire, the Austro-Hungarian Empire, the Ottoman Empire or the British Empire. They survived for long periods of time and endured many political changes because their feudal basis enabled them to distribute power flexibly over a wide range of smaller, secondary power centres.

NATION-STATE AND POWER

With the appearance of the nation-state, trade, commerce and finance pushed for political participation and subsequently added their power to traditional state structures. The development of the nation-state at the beginning of the Industrial Revolution more than 200 years ago went hand in hand with the unregulated accumulation of capital on the one hand and the unhindered exploitation of a fast-growing population on the other hand. The new bourgeoisie which rose from this revolution wanted to take part in political decisions and state structures. Capitalism, their new economic system, thus became an inherent component of the new nation-state. The nation-state needed the bourgeoisie and the power of capital in order to replace the old feudal order and its ideology, which rested on tribal structures and inherited rights, with a new national ideology that united all tribes and clans under the roof of the nation. In this way, capitalism and nation-state became so closely linked to each other that neither could be imagined as existing without the other. As a consequence, exploitation was not only sanctioned by the state but even encouraged and facilitated.

But above all the nation-state must be thought as the maximum form of power. None of the other types of state have such a capacity for power. One of the main reasons for this is that the upper part of the middle class has been linked to the process of monopolisation in an ever-increasing manner. The nation-state itself is the most developed and complete monopoly. It is the most advanced unity of monopolies such as trade, industry, finance and power. One should also think of ideological monopoly as an indivisible part of the power monopoly.

THE STATE AND ITS RELIGIOUS ROOTS

The religious roots of the state have already been discussed in detail.[1] Many contemporary political concepts and notions have their origin in religious or theological concepts or structures. In fact, a closer look reveals that religion and divine imagination brought about the first social identities in history. They formed the ideological glue

---

1   A. Öcalan, *The Roots of Civilisation*, London, 2007.

of many tribes and other pre-state communities and defined their existence as communities.

Later, after state structures had already developed, the traditional links between state, power and society began to weaken. The sacred and divine ideas and practices which had been present when the community began increasingly lost their meaning in relation to a common identity and were, instead, transferred to the power structures of monarchs or dictators. The state and its power were derived from divine will and law and its ruler became king by the grace of God. They represented divine power on earth.

Today, most modern states call themselves secular, claiming that the old bonds between religion and state have been severed and that religion is no longer a part of the state. This is arguably only a half truth. Even if religious institutions or representatives of the clergy no longer participate in political and social decision-making they still influence these decisions to an extent, just as they are influenced themselves by political or social ideas and developments. Therefore, secularism, or laicism as it is called in Turkey, still contains religious elements. The separation of state and religion is the result of a political decision. It did not come naturally. This is why even today power and state seem to be given, God-given we might even say. Notions like *secular state* or *secular power* remain ambiguous.

The nation-state has also allocated a number of attributes which serve to replace older, religiously rooted attributes like nation, fatherland, national flag, national anthem and many others. Particularly notions like *the unity of state and nation* serve to transcend the material political structures and are, as such, reminiscent of the pre-state *unity with God.* They have replaced the *divine.*

When in former times a tribe subjugated another tribe its members had to worship the gods of the victors. We may arguably call this process a process of colonisation, even assimilation. The nation-state is a centralised state with quasi-divine attributes that has completely disarmed society and monopolises the use of force.

BUREAUCRACY AND THE NATION-STATE

Since the nation-state transcends its material basis – the citizens – it assumes an existence beyond its political institutions. It needs additional institutions of its own to protect its ideological basis as well as legal, economic and religious structures. The resulting ever-expanding civil and military bureaucracy is expensive and serves only the preservation of the transcendent state itself, which in turn elevates the bureaucracy above the people.

During European modernity, the state had the means necessary to expand its bureaucracy into all strata of society. There it grew like a cancer, infecting all societal lifelines. Bureaucracy and the nation-state cannot exist without each other. If the nation-state is the backbone of capitalist modernity it is certainly the cage of natural society. Its bureaucracy secures the smooth functioning of the system, secures the basis of the production of goods, and secures profits for the relevant economic actors in both the real socialist and business-friendly nation-state. The nation-state domesticates society in the name of capitalism and alienates the community from its natural foundations. Any analysis meant to localise and solve social problems needs to take a close look at these links.

NATION-STATE AND HOMOGENEITY

The nation-state in its original form aimed at the monopolisation of all social processes. Diversity and plurality had to be fought, an approach that led to assimilation and genocide. It not only exploits the ideas and the labour potential of society, and colonises people's heads in the name of capitalism. It also assimilates all kinds of spiritual and intellectual ideas and cultures in order to preserve its own existence. It aims at creating a single national culture, a single national identity and a single unified religious community. Thus it also enforces a homogeneous citizenship. The notion of citizen has been created as a result of the quest for such a homogeneity. The citizenship of modernity defines nothing but the transition made from private slavery to state slavery. Capitalism cannot attain profit in the absence of such modern slave armies. The homogenic national society is the most artificial society to have ever been created and is the result of a 'social engineering project'.

These goals are generally accomplished by the use of force or by financial incentives, and have often resulted in the physical annihilation of minorities, cultures or languages, or in forced assimilation. The history of the last two centuries is full of examples illustrating the violent attempts at creating a nation that corresponds to the imaginary reality of a true nation-state.

NATION-STATE AND SOCIETY

It is often said that the nation-state is concerned with the fate of the common people. This is not true. Rather, it is the national governor of the worldwide capitalist system, a vassal of capitalist modernity which is more deeply entangled in the dominant structures of capital than we tend to assume: it is a colony for capital. Regardless of how nationalist the nation-state may present itself, to the same extent it serves the capitalist processes of exploitation. There is no other explanation for the horrible redistribution wars of capitalist modernity. Thus the nation-state is not with the common people – it is an enemy of the people.

Relations between other nation-states and international monopolies are coordinated by the diplomats of the nation-state. Without the recognition of other nation-states none of them could survive. The reason can be found in the logic of the worldwide capitalist system. Nation-states which leave the phalanx of the capitalist system are overtaken by the same fate that the Saddam regime in Iraq experienced, or it will be brought to its knees by means of economic embargoes.

Let us now derive some characteristics of the nation-state from the example of the Republic of Turkey.

Ideological Foundations of the Nation-State

In the past, the history of states was often equated with the history of their rulers, which lent them almost divine qualities. This practice changed with the rise of the nation-state. Now the entire state became idealised and elevated to a divine level.

NATIONALISM

Assuming that we would compare the nation-state to a living god, then nationalism would be the correspondent religion. In spite of some seemingly positive elements, nation-state and nationalism show metaphysical characteristics. In this context, capitalist profit and the accumulation of capital appear as categories shrouded in mystery. There is a network of contradictory relations behind these terms that is based on force and exploitation. Their hegemonic striving for power serves the maximisation of profits. In this sense, nationalism appears as a quasi-religious justification. Its true mission, however, is its service to the virtually divine nation-state and its ideological vision which pervades all areas of the society. Arts, science and social awareness: none of them is independent. A true intellectual enlightenment therefore needs a fundamental analysis of these elements of modernity.

POSITIVIST SCIENCE

The paradigm of a positivist or descriptive science forms another ideological pillar of the nation-state. It fuels nationalist ideology but also laicism, which has taken the form of a new religion. On the other hand, it is one of the ideological foundations of modernity and its dogmata have had a pervasive influence on the social sciences.

Positivism can be circumscribed as a philosophical approach that is strictly confined to the appearance of things, which it equates with reality itself. Since in positivism appearance is reality, anything that doesn't have an appearance cannot be part of reality. We know from quantum physics, astronomy, some fields of biology and even the gist of thought itself that reality occurs in worlds that are beyond observable events. The truth, in the relationship between the observed and the observer, has mystified itself to the extent that it no longer fits any physical scale or definition. Positivism denies this, and therefore to an extent resembles the idol-worshipping of ancient times, where the idol constitutes the image of reality.

SEXISM

Another ideological pillar of the nation-state is the sexism that pervades entire societies. Many civilised systems have employed sexism in order to preserve their own power. They enforced women's exploitation and used them as a valuable reservoir of cheap labour. Women are also regarded as a valuable resource in so far as they produce offspring and allow the reproduction of men. Thus, a woman is both a sexual object and a commodity. She is a tool for the preservation of male power and can at best advance to become an accessory of the patriarchal male society.

On the one hand, the sexism of the society of the nation-state strengthens the power of men; on the other hand, the nation-state turns its society into a colony through the exploitation of women. In this respect women can also be regarded as an exploited nation.

In the course of the history of civilisation the patriarchy consolidated the traditional framework of hierarchies, which in the nation-state is fuelled by sexism. Socially rooted sexism is just like nationalism: an ideological product of the nation-state and of power. Socially rooted sexism is not less dangerous than capitalism. The patriarchy, however, tries to hide these facts. This is understandable given the fact that all power relations and state ideologies are fuelled by sexist concepts and behaviour. Without the repression of women the repression of an entire society is inconceivable. Sexism within the nation-state on the one hand gives men maximum power, while on the other hand turns society, through women, into the worst colony of all. Hence woman is the historical society's colony nation which has reached its worst position within the nation-state. All the power and state ideologies stem from sexist attitudes and behaviour. Woman's slavery is the most profound and disguised social area where all types of slavery, oppression and colonisation are realised. Capitalism and nation-state act in full awareness of this. Without woman's slavery none of the other types of slavery can exist, let alone develop. Capitalism and nation-state denote the most institutionalised dominant male. More boldly and openly spoken: capitalism and nation-state are the monopolism of the despotic and exploitative male.

RELIGIOUSNESS

Even if it acts seemingly like a secular state, the nation-state does not shy away from using a mélange of nationalism and religion for its purposes. The reason is simple: religion still plays an important part in some societies or parts of them. Islam is particularly agile in this respect.

However, religion in the age of modernity no longer plays its traditional role. Whether it is radical or moderate belief, religion in the nation-state no longer has a mission in society. It can only do what it is permitted by the nation-state. Its still existing influence and its functionality, which can be misused for the promotion of nationalism, are interesting aspects for the nation-state. In some cases religion even takes on the part of nationalism. The Shi'ah of Iran is one of the most powerful ideological weapons of the Iranian state. In Turkey the Sunni ideology plays a similar but more limited role.

The Kurds and the Nation-State

After the preceding short introduction to the nation-state and its basic ideology, we will now see why the foundation of a separate Kurdish nation-state does not make sense for the Kurds.

Over the last decades the Kurds have not only struggled against repression by the dominant powers and for the recognition of their existence, but also for the liberation of their society from the grip of feudalism. Hence it does not make sense to replace the old chains with new ones or even enhance the repression. This is what the foundation of a nation-state would mean in the context of capitalist modernity. Without opposition against capitalist modernity there will be no place for the liberation of the people. This is why the founding of a Kurdish nation-state is not an option for me.

The call for a separate nation-state results from the interests of the ruling class or the interests of the bourgeoisie, but does not reflect the interests of the people since another state would only be the creation of additional injustice and would curtail the right to freedom even more.

The solution to the Kurdish question, therefore, needs to be found in an approach that weakens capitalist modernity or pushes it back. There are historical reasons, social peculiarities and actual developments, as well as the fact that the settlement area of the Kurds extends over the territories of four different countries, which make a democratic solution indispensable. Furthermore, there is also the important fact that the entire Middle East suffers from a democracy deficit. Thanks to the geostrategic situation of the Kurdish settlement area, successful Kurdish democratic projects promise to advance the democratisation of the Middle East in general. Let us call this democratic project *democratic confederalism*.

DEMOCRATIC CONFEDERALISM

This kind of rule or administration can be called a non-state political administration, or democracy without a state. Democratic decision-making processes must not be confused with the processes known from public administration. States only administrate, while democracies govern. States are founded on power; democracies are based on collective consensus. Office in the state is determined by decree, even though it may in part be legitimised by elections. Democracies use direct elections. The state uses coercion as a legitimate means. Democracies rest on voluntary participation.

Democratic confederalism is open towards other political groups and factions. It is flexible, multicultural, anti-monopolistic and consensus-oriented. Ecology and feminism are central pillars. In the frame of this kind of self-governance an alternative economy will become necessary, which increases the resources of the society instead of exploiting them and thus does justice to the manifold needs of the society.

Participation and the Diversity of the Political Landscape

The contradictory composition of society necessitates political groups with both vertical and horizontal formations. Central, regional and local groups need to be balanced in this way. Only they, each representing itself, are able to deal with their special concrete situations and develop appropriate solutions for far-reaching social problems. It is a natural right to express one's cultural, ethnic or national identity with the help of political associations. However, this right needs an ethical and political society. Whether nation-state, republic or democracy – democratic confederalism is open to compromises concerning state or governmental traditions. It allows for equal coexistence.

The Heritage of Society and the Accumulation of Historical Knowledge

Then again, democratic confederalism rests on the historical experience of society and its collective heritage. It is not an arbitrary modern political system but, rather, accumulates history and experience. It is the offspring of the life of the society.

The state continuously orientates itself towards centralism in order to pursue the interests of power monopolies. The opposite is true for confederalism. Not monopolies but society is at the centre of political focus. The heterogeneous structure of society is in contradiction to all forms of centralism. Distinct centralism only results in social eruptions.

Within living memory, people have always formed loose groups of clans, tribes or other communities with federal qualities. In this way they were able to preserve their internal autonomy. Even the internal government of empires employed diverse methods of self-administration for their different parts, which included religious authorities, tribal councils, kingdoms and even republics. Hence it is important to understand that even empires which appear centralist follow a confederate organisational structure. The centralist model is not an administrative system wanted by society. Instead, it is an administrative model required by the monopolies.

Moral and Political Society

The classification of society into categories and terms following a certain pattern is produced artificially by capitalist monopolies. Such societies do not exist. Their propaganda does. However, societies are essentially political and moral. Economic, political, ideological and military monopolies are constructions which contradict the nature of society by merely striving for the accumulation of surplus. They do not create values. Nor can a revolution create a new society. It can only play a positive role in restoring the moral and political fabric of the society that has been eroded. The rest is determined by the free will of moral and political society.

I mentioned already that capitalist modernity enforces the centralisation of the state. The political and military power centres within society have been deprived of their influence. The nation-state as a modern substitute for monarchy left a weakened and defenceless society behind. In this respect, legal order and public peace only imply the class rule of the bourgeoisie. Power constitutes itself in the central state and becomes one of the fundamental administrative paradigms of modernity. This means the nation-state exists in contrast to democracy and republicanism.

Our project of 'democratic modernity' is meant as an alternative draft to modernity as we know it. It builds on democratic confederalism as a fundamental political paradigm. Democratic modernity is the roof of the moral and political society. As long as we make the mistake of believing that societies need to be homogeneous monolithic entities it will be difficult to understand democratic confederalism. Modernity's history is also a history of four centuries of cultural and physical genocide in the name of an imaginary unitary society. Democratic confederalism, on the other hand, is self-defence against this history and the history of insisting on multi-ethnic, multicultural and different political formations.

The crisis of the financial system is an inherent consequence of the capitalist nation-state. However, all efforts of the neoliberals to change the nation-state have remained unsuccessful. The Middle East provides instructive examples.

Democratic Confederalism and Democratic Politics

In contrast to *the nation-state*'s centralist, linear and bureaucratic understanding of administration and *the* exercise of power, democratic confederalism poses a type of political formation where society governs itself and where all societal groups and cultural identities can express themselves in local meetings, general conventions and councils. What is important is the ability to take decisions through councils and discussions. Administration that is elite and not grounded in these are deemed invalid. Democratic governance and supervision of societal work is done through clusters of councils that are multi-structured and strive for unity in diversity, whether they be the general central coordination councils (like assemblies, commissions or congresses) or local councils.

Democratic society is the way to build democratic confederalism. This is where its democraticness stems from. Capitalist modernity destroys political space, as it attempts to maintain itself through power and state apparatuses that become ever-more centralised and spread into the fabric of society. Therefore democratic politics, by giving different sections and identities within society the opportunity to express themselves and become political forces, reforms political society at the same time. Politics becomes a part of social life once again. Without politics, the crisis of the state cannot be solved, since it is fuelled by the denial of political society.

Democratic confederalism not only has the potential to overcome the problems originating from the nation-state systematic, it is also the most appropriate tool with which to politicise society. It is simple and implementable. Each community, ethnicity, culture, religious community, intellectual movement, economic unit, etc., can autonomously configure and express themselves as a political unit.

Whether federate or autonomous, the concept of the self should be seen in this framework and scope. Each self has the chance to form a confederation from the local to the global. The most fundamental factor of the local is the right to free discussion and the right to make decisions. Each self or federate unit is unique because it has the chance to implement direct democracy, which can also be called participative democracy. Its strength is drawn from the feasibility of direct democracy. This is another reason why it has a fundamental role. While the nation-state is in contrast with, and even in denial of, direct democracy, democratic confederalism is the form where direct democracy is constituted and becomes functional.

Thus, just as the nation-state oppresses, homogenises and distances society from democracy, the democratic confederalist model liberates, diversifies and democratises.

The federate units, which are stem cells of direct and participative democracy, are also unique and ideal because they have the flexibility to transform into confederate units if required. Any political unit, if based on units that rest on direct and participative democracy, is democratic. It is thus possible to call this political functionality, developed in a local unit or as a global formation, democratic politics. A true democratic system is the formulation of experiencing all these processes. It is thus important to understand that confederate units are needed even in a village, or on a street in any city. For example, direct democracy units such as the ecologic unit or federate of the village, together with the free women's unit, self-defence, youth, education, arts, health, solidarity and economic units, should unite. This new unit can easily be called a confederate unit or union. As this system is applied at a local, regional, national and global level it can easily be seen what an inclusive system democratic confederalism is.

Democratic Confederalism and Self-Defence

Essentially, the nation-state is a militarily structured entity. Nation-states are eventually the products of all kinds of internal and external warfare. None of the existing nation-states has come into existence all by itself. Invariably, they have a record of wars. This process is not limited to their founding phase but, rather, it builds on the militarisation of an entire society. The civil leadership of the state is only an accessory of the military apparatus. Liberal democracies even outdo this by painting their militaristic structures in democratic and liberal colours. However, this doesn't keep them from seeking authoritarian solutions at the highpoint of a crisis caused by the system itself. The fascist exercise of power is the nature of the nation-state. Fascism is the purest form of the nation-state.

This militarisation can only be pushed back with the help of self-defence. Societies without any mechanism for self-defence lose their identities, their capability of democratic decision-making, and their political nature. Therefore, the self-defence of a society is not limited to the military dimension alone. It also presupposes the preservation of its identity, its own political awareness, and a process of democratisation. Only then can we talk about self-defence.

Against this background, democratic confederalism can be called a system of self-defence of society. Self-defence can only respond to hegemony if it is based on democratic politics and its own system is based on confederal networks. Just as there are many hegemonic networks and gangs (commercial, financial, industrial, power, nation-state and ideological monopolies) there should be as many confederal, self-defence and democratic politics networks developed.

This means in particular that the social paradigm of confederalism does not involve a military monopoly for the armed forces, which have the sole task of ensuring internal and external security. They are under direct control of democratic institutions. Society itself must be able to determine their duties. One of their tasks will be the defence of the free will of society from internal and external interventions. The commanding structures of the units should be under the double supervision of both the organs of democratic politics and the members of each unit themselves. If the need arises to make and accept proposals, changes can easily be made.

Democratic Confederalism versus Striving for Hegemony

In democratic confederalism there is no room for any kind of hegemony striving. This is particularly true in the field of ideology. Hegemony is a principle that is usually followed by the classic type of civilisation. Democratic civilisations reject hegemonic powers and ideologies. Any ways of expression which cut across the boundaries of democratic self-governance would carry self-governance and freedom of expression *ad absurdum*. The collective handling of societal matters requires understanding, respect for dissenting opinions and democratic decision-making mechanisms. This is in contrast to the understanding of governance in capitalist modernity, where the arbitrary bureaucratic decisions that characterise the nation-state are diametrically opposed to democratic civilisation and modernity's understanding of governance that act in line with moral foundations. In democratic confederalism, leadership institutions do not need ideological legitimisation. Hence, they need not strive for hegemony.

World Democratic Confederal Union

Although in democratic confederalism the focus is on the local level, organising confederalism globally is not excluded. Contrariwise, we need to put up a platform of national civil societies in terms of a World Democratic Confederal Union to oppose the United Nations as an association of nation-states under the leadership of the superpowers. It is necessary to bring together wide-ranging communities within a World Democratic Confederation if we want a more secure, peaceful, ecologic, just and productive world.

Conclusion

Democratic confederalism can be described as a kind of self-governance in contrast to administration by the nation-state. The relationship between a democratic confederation and nation-states should neither be continuous warfare nor assimilation of the former into the latter. It is a relationship of principles that rests on the acceptance of two separate entities that accept coexistence. In the case of interventions and attacks, not only by nation-states but in general from capitalist modernity, democratic confederations should always have self-defence forces.

Democratic confederalism is not at war with any nation-state but it will not stand idly by while assimilation efforts take place. Revolutionary overthrow or the foundation of a new state does not create sustainable change. In the long run, freedom and justice can only be accomplished within a democratic-confederate dynamic process.

Neither total rejection nor complete recognition of the state is useful for the democratic efforts of civil society. The overcoming of the state, particularly the nation-state, is a long-term process.

The state will be overcome when democratic confederalism has proved its problem-solving capacities with a view to social issues. This does not mean, though, that attacks by nation-states have to be accepted. Democratic confederations will sustain self-defence forces at all times. Democratic confederations will not be limited to organising themselves within a single particular territory. They will become cross-border confederations when the societies concerned so desire.

PRINCIPLES OF DEMOCRATIC CONFEDERALISM

1. The right of self-determination of the people includes the right to a state of their own. However, the foundation of a state does not increase the freedom of a people. The system of the United Nations that is based on nation-states has remained inefficient. Meanwhile, nation-states have become serious obstacles for any social development. Democratic confederalism is the contrasting paradigm of the oppressed people.

2. Democratic confederalism is a non-state social paradigm. It is not controlled by a state. At the same time, democratic confederalism is the organisation of democracy and culture.

3. Democratic confederalism is based on grassroots participation. Its decision-making processes lie with the communities. Higher levels only serve the coordination and implementation of the will of the communities that send their delegates to the general assemblies. For one year they are both mouthpiece and executive institutions. However, the basic decision-making power rests with the local grassroots institutions.

4. In the Middle East, democracy cannot be imposed by the capitalist system and its imperial powers, which only damage democracy. The propagation of grassroots democracy is elementary. It is the only approach that can cope with diverse ethnic groups, religions and class differences. It also goes together well with the traditional confederal structure of the society.

5. Democratic confederalism in Kurdistan is also an anti-nationalist movement. It aims at realising the right of self-defence of the people by the advancement of democracy in all parts of Kurdistan without questioning existing political borders. Its goal is not the foundation of a Kurdish nation-state. The movement intends to establish federal structures in Iran, Turkey, Syria and Iraq that are open to all Kurds and at the same time form an umbrella confederation for all four parts of Kurdistan.

PROBLEMS OF THE PEOPLES IN THE MIDDLE EAST AND POSSIBLE WAYS TO A SOLUTION

The national question is not a phantasm of capitalist modernity. Nevertheless it was capitalist modernity which imposed the national question on society. The national society replaced religious community. However, the transition to a national society needs to overcome capitalist modernity if the nation is not to remain a disguise for repressive monopolies.

Despite the overemphasis of the nation in the Middle East having a negative effect, ignoring the national aspect of society would also aggravate the problem. Hence the method in handling the issue should not be ideological but scientific, and not nation-statist but based on the concept of the democratic nation and democratic communalism. The contents of such an approach are the fundamental elements of democratic entities.

Over the past two centuries, nationalism and the tendency towards nation-states have been fuelled in the societies of the Middle East. National issues have not been solved but rather have been aggravated in all areas of society. Instead of cultivating productive competition, capital enforces internal and external wars in the name of the nation-state.

The theory of socialist communalism would be an alternative to capitalism. In the framework of the democratic nation, which does not strive for power monopolies, it may lead to peace in a region which has only been the setting for gory wars and genocides.

In this context we can speak of four majority nations: Arabs, Persians, Turks and Kurds. I do not wish to divide nations into majority or minority as I do not find this to be appropriate. But due to demographic considerations I shall speak of majority nations. In the same context we may also use the term minority nations.

1. There are more than 20 Arab nation-states which divide the Arab community and damage their societies by wars. This is one of the main factors responsible for the alienation of cultural values and the apparent hopelessness of the Arab national question, which continuously shatter the Arab community, alienate them from their own values, exhaust them through wars and consume their material wealth. These nation-states have not even been able to form a confederalism between themselves. They are the main reason of the problematic situation of the Arab nation. A religiously motivated tribal nationalism together with a sexist patriarchal society pervades all areas of society, resulting in distinct conservatism and slavish obedience. This situation does not give the opportunity to pose any questions – whether domestic or international – to be resolved in

the name of the Arabs. However, a model based on the democratic nation and socialist communality might provide such a solution. The strength of Israel, which the Arab nation-states regard as a competitor, is not only the result of international support by the hegemonic powers. The strong internal democratic and communal institutions within Israel have an important role to play in this. Over the last century, the society of the Arab nation has been weakened by radical nationalism and Islamism. Yet, if they are able to unite communal socialism (which they are not a stranger to) with that of the understanding of a democratic nation, then they may be able to find themselves a secure, long-term solution.

2. The Turks and Turkmens form another majority nation. They share an understanding of power and ideology with the Arabs. They are strict nation-statists and have a profound religious and racial nationalism engraved in them. From a sociological point of view, the Turks and Turkmens are quite different. The relations between Turkmens and Turkish aristocracy resemble the tensed relations between Bedouins and Arab aristocracy. They form a stratum whose interests are compatible with democracy and communalism. The Turkish national problems are quite complex. The striving for power of the nation-state, excessively religious and ethnic nationalism and a sexist patriarchal society prevail and create a very conservative society. It is as if society, democracy and communal tendencies are disintegrated within extreme statist and hegemonic ideological monopolies. The family is regarded as the smallest cell of the state, not that of society. Both individuals and institutions imitate the state. These historical tendencies lead to a harsh struggle for power between the Turks and Turkmens communities. Similar power struggles are also experienced within societies due to this politics of conquest. The centralist power structures of the Turkish nation-state and its rigid official ideology have prevented democratic and communal tendencies from developing and resolving the Turkish national question. The message sent to society is that it is not possible to live without the state. There is no balance between

society/the individual and the state. Obedience is regarded as the greatest virtue.

In contrast to this, the theory of democratic modernity offers an adequate framework for Turkish national communities. A community-based project of a democratic Turkish confederation would both strengthen its internal unity and create the conditions for a peaceful coexistence with the neighbours that it lives with. Borders have lost their former meaning when it comes to social unity. In spite of geographic boundaries, today's modern communication tools allow for a virtual unity between individuals and communities wherever they are. A democratic confederation of Turkish national communities could be a contribution to world peace and the system of democratic modernity.

3. Kurdish national society stems from the rich potential that is newly developing as a result of their struggle. Worldwide, they are the most populous people without a nation-state. They have been living in their present, strategic settlement areas since the Neolithic period. Agriculture and stock breeding, as well as their readiness to defend themselves using the geographic advantages of their mountainous homeland, helped the Kurds to survive as a native people. The Kurdish national question rises from the fact that they have been denied their right to nationhood. Others tried to assimilate them, annihilate them, and in the end flatly denied their existence. Not having a state of their own has advantages and disadvantages. The excrescences of state-based civilisations have only been taken in to a limited extent. This can be a benefit in the realisation of democratic modernity that goes beyond capitalist modernity. Their settlement area is divided by the national borders of four countries and lies in a geostrategically important region, thus providing the Kurds with a strategic advantage. The Kurds do not have the option of forming a national society through the use of state power. The elements of capitalist modernity can not offer much in this sense. Although there is a Kurdish political entity today in Iraqi-Kurdistan, it is not a nation-state but rather a parastatal entity.

Kurdistan has also been home to Armenian and Aramaic minorities as well as other peoples in the recent past. There are also smaller groups of Arab, Persian and Turkic groups that have settled in the area. Even today there are many different religions and faiths living side by side in this region. There also strong traces of a clan and tribal culture, although urban culture has not developed much.

All these properties are a blessing for new democratic political formations. Communal units in farming but also in the areas of water and energy are not only ideal but necessary. The situation is also favourable for the development of moral and political society. Even the patriarchal ideology is less deeply rooted here than in neighbouring societies. This is beneficial for the establishment of a democratic society where women's freedom and equality are to form one of the main pillars. It also offers the conditions for the creation of a democratic nation and ecologic and economic society in line with the paradigm of democratic modernity. The project of the Kurdistan Democratic Confederation already has an opportunity to be implemented. The construction of a democratic nation based on multinational identities is the ideal solution when faced with the nation-state dead-end street. The emerging entity could become a blueprint for the entire Middle East and expand dynamically into neighbouring countries. Convincing neighbouring nations of this model could change the fate of the Middle East and would reinforce the possibility of democratic modernity creating an alternative. In this sense, therefore, the freedom, equality and democratic development of the Kurds and Kurdistan would be synonymous with the freedom, equality and democracy of the region and its peoples.

4. The reasons for today's problems of the Persian or Iranian nation can be found in the interventions of historical civilisations and capitalist modernity. Although their original identity was a result of the Zoroastrian and Mithraic traditions, these have been annulled by a derivative of Islam. Manichaeism, which emerged as a synthesis of Judaism, Christianity and Mohammedanism with Greek philosophy, was not able to prevail against the ideology of the official civilisation. Indeed, it went no further then to nurture the

tradition of rebellion. It has hence converted the Islamic tradition into Shi'ah denomination and adopted it to be its latest civilisational ideology. Presently, efforts are being made to modernise itself by passing the elements of capitalist modernity through its Shi'ah filter.

Iranian society is multi-ethnic and multi-religious and blessed with a rich culture. All the national and religious identities of the Middle East can be found there. This diversity is in contrast to the hegemonic claim of the theocracy, which cultivates a subtle religious and ethnic nationalism; the ruling class does not shrink back from anti-modernist propaganda whenever it serves their interests, although they implement capitalist modernity. Revolutionary and democratic tendencies have been integrated by the traditional civilisation. A despotic regime skilfully governs the country. It heads the list of states and societies that are the most tense and which contain many contradictions. Although the petrol revenues partially soothe the tensions, Iranian nation-statism exists at a point where it is most open to disintegration. The frictions between itself and the US-EU hegemonic powers have had an effect on this.

Despite strong centralist efforts in Iran, it is as if there is also a federal Iran at the grassroots level. When elements of democratic civilisation and federalist elements including Azeris, Kurds, Baluchis, Arabs and Turkmens intersect, the project of a 'Democratic Confederation of Iran' can emerge and become attractive. Women's movement and communal traditions will play a special role here.

5. The Armenian national question is a leading tragedy that has been caused by the entrance of capitalist modernity into the Middle East. The Armenians are one of the most ancient peoples in the region. They shared much of their settlement area with the Kurds. While the Kurds lived primarily on agriculture and animal husbandry, the Armenians nurtured and were nurtured by this economy through arts and crafts in the towns. Although they have a resistance similar to that of the Kurds, they never had permanent state institutions. The Armenians were the first people to adopt Christianity. Identity and belief in redemption play an

important role in this. The instrumentalisation of the Armenians by capitalist modernity in their desire to enter the Middle East was a strategic mistake. Their entrapment under the Muslim majority because of their Christianity eventually turned into a tragedy due to nation-state nationalism. Armenians who made huge contributions to Middle Eastern culture became the victim of a terrible catastrophe as a result of the plots staged by capitalist modernity.

Apart from the Jews, the Armenians are the second-largest people to live primarily in the diaspora. The foundation of an Armenian state to the west of Azerbaijan, however, does not mean that the Armenian national question is resolved. The consequences of the genocide can hardly be remedied. They shall always continue to search for the homeland that they have lost. Therefore the present-day Armenian question is defined by trying to find the homeland that they have lost. There are other peoples living in the homeland that they search for. Any concepts based on a nation-state cannot offer a solution. There is neither a homogenous population structure there nor any clear borders, as is required by capitalist modernity. The thinking of their opponents may be fascist; however, it is not enough to only explore the reasons that are related to them, it is also vital that they focus on new ways out of the situation. Confederate structures could be an alternative for the Armenians. In the event that they renew themselves under the Armenian democratic nation, not only shall they continue to play their historical role within Middle Eastern culture, but they shall find the right path to liberation.

6. In modern times the Christian Arameans (Assyrians) also suffered the fate of the Armenians. It is a huge loss for Middle Eastern culture. They too are one of the oldest peoples in the Middle East. They were not only the initial creators of Christianity but also of the trade monopoly within Middle Eastern civilisation. Their instrumentalisation by capitalist modernity would lead to a similar fate to that of the Armenians. They shared a settlement area with the Kurds but also with other people. Their sad ending was prepared by the deepening of their isolation due to Christianity with that of capitalist modernity. The catastrophie that befell both peoples

was not only due to the fascist, genocidal actions of the Turkish Committee of Unity and Progress – the collaborationist Kurds also played an important role in this. The question of Aramean national society has its roots in patriarchal civilisation, but has also developed further with Christianity and ideologies of modernity. In order for there to be a solution, there needs to be a radical transformation of the Arameans. Their real salvation may be to break away from the mentality of classical civilisation and capitalist modernity, and instead embrace democratic civilisation and renew their rich cultural memory as an element of democratic modernity, in order to reconstruct themselves as the 'Aramean Democratic Nation'.

7. The Jewish question is as much a world question as it is a Middle Eastern societal problem. The history of the Jewish people also gives expression to the problematic cultural history of the Middle East. The search for the backdrop of expulsion, pogroms and genocide amounts to sitting in judgement on civilisations. The Jewish community has taken up the influences of the old Sumerian and Egyptian cultures, as well as those of regional tribal cultures. They have skilfully reformed these cultural resources to transform them into their Jewish tribal culture. It has contributed a lot to the culture of the Middle East. Like the Arameans, they fell victim to the traditions of civilisation and capitalist modernity that they helped create. They too should try and find a solution for themselves in the elements of democratic modernity that I have tried to develop. No doubt intellectuals of Jewish descent have progressive views in this direction. However, this is nowhere near enough. For a solution of the problems as they exist today, a renewed appropriation of the history of the Middle East is needed on a democratic basis. In a nation-statist Middle East, Israel will necessarily be continuously at war. The slogan is: 'an eye for an eye'. Fire can not be put out by fire. Although it may bolster Israel's confidence to find the hegemonic power of capitalist modernity behind it, this is not enough for a deep-rooted solution. The Israel-Palestine conflict makes it clear that the nation-state paradigm is not helpful in providing a solution, but aggravates the problem.

There has been much bloodshed and money spent; what remains is the difficult legacy of seemingly irresolvable problems. The Israel-Palestine example shows the complete failure of capitalist modernity and the nation-state.

The Jews belong to the culture bearers of the Middle East. Their denial and genocides is a loss for everyone. Their transformation into a democratic nation, just as for Armenians and Arameans, would make their participation in a democratic confederation of the Middle East easier. The project of an 'East-Aegean Democratic Confederation' would be a positive start. Strict and exclusive national and religious identities may evolve into flexible and open identities under this project. Israel may also evolve into a more acceptable, open democratic nation. Undoubtedly though, its neighbours must also go through such a transformation.

Tensions and armed conflicts in the Middle East make a transformation of the paradigm of modernity seem inevitable. Without it a solution to such difficult social problems and national questions is impossible. Democratic modernity offers an alternative to the system that is unable to resolve these problems.

8. The annihilation of Hellenic culture in Anatolia is a loss that cannot be compensated. In the first quarter of the twentieth century the reciprocal forced migrations by the Turkish and Greek nation-states had an impact as painful as the genocides. No state has the right to drive people from their ancestral cultural region. Nevertheless, the nation-states showed their inhuman approach towards such issues again and again. The attacks on the Hellenic, Jewish, Aramean and Armenian cultures were stepped up, while Islam spread throughout the Middle East. This, in turn, contributed to the decline of Middle Eastern civilisation. Islamic culture has never been able to fill the emerging void. In the nineteenth century, when capitalist modernity advanced into the Middle East it found a cultural desert created by self-inflicted cultural erosion. Cultural diversity also strengthens the defence mechanism of a society. Monocultures are less robust. Hence, the conquest of the Middle East was not difficult. The project of a homogeneous nation as

propagated by the nation-state bears the utmost responsibility for the cultural genocides.

9. Caucasian ethnic groups also have social problems which are not insignificant. Again and again, they have migrated into the Middle East and stimulated its cultures. They have unquestionably contributed to its cultural wealth. The arrival of modernity almost made these minority cultures disappear. They, too, would find an acceptable place in a confederal structure.

Finally, let me state again that the fundamental problems of the Middle East are deeply rooted in classed and state civilisation. These fundamental social problems in the Middle East have become more aggravated together with the structural global crisis. The regional agents of dominant modernity are not even aware of what they are representing, let alone able to define what the questions and their solutions are. The elements of democratic modernity that I have tried to define represent the theoretical and practical forces that can stop the genocides and defend life. When these forces – on the basis of democratic, economic and ecologic society – make the transition to the Age of Democratic Nations, life can return to its former enchantment within the Middle Eastern culture.

3

Liberating Life:
Woman's Revolution

INTRODUCTION

The question of women's freedom has intrigued me throughout my life. While at first I viewed the enslavement of women in the Middle East and in general as the result of feudal backwardness, after many years of revolutionary practice and research I came to the conclusion that the problem goes much deeper. The 5,000-year-old history of civilisation is essentially the history of the enslavement of woman. Consequently, woman's freedom will only be achieved by waging a struggle against the foundations of this ruling system.

An analysis of mainstream civilisation with regard to the freedom question will make it clear that civilisation has been weighted down by an ever-increasing slavery. This 'mainstream civilisation' is the civilisation passed down from, and in return influenced by, Sumer to Akkad, from Babylon to Assur, from Persia to Greece, Rome, Byzantium, Europe and finally the USA. Throughout the long history of this civilisation, slavery has been perpetuated on three levels. First, there is the construction of ideological slavery (conspicuously, but understandably, fearsome and dominant gods are constructed from mythologies); then there is use of force; lastly, there is seizure of the economy.

This three-tiered enchainment of society is well-illustrated by the ziggurats, the temples established by the Sumerian priest-state. The upper levels of the ziggurats are propounded as the quarters of the god who controls the mind. The middle floors are the political and administrative headquarters of the priests. Finally, the bottom floor houses the craftsmen and agricultural workers who are forced to work in all kinds of production. Essentially, this model has been unchanged until today. Thus, an analysis of the ziggurat is in fact an analysis of the continuous mainstream civilisation system that will enable us to analyse the current capitalist world system in terms of its true basis. Continuous, accumulative development of capital and power is only one side of the medallion. The other side is horrendous slavery, hunger, poverty and coercion into a herd-like society.

Without depriving society of its freedom and ensuring that it can be managed like a herd, central civilisation[1] cannot sustain or preserve itself, because of the nature of the system according to which it functions. This is done by creating even more capital and instruments of power, causing ever-increasing poverty and a herd-like mentality. The reason why the issue of freedom is the key question in every age, lies in the nature of the system itself.

The history of the loss of freedom is at the same time the history of how woman lost her position and vanished from history. It is the history of how the dominant male, with all his gods and servants, rulers and subordinates, his economy, science and arts, obtained power. Woman's downfall and loss is thus the downfall and loss of the whole of civilisation, with the sexist society that resulted. The sexist male is so keen on constructing his social dominance over woman that he turns any contact with her into a show of dominance.

The depth of woman's enslavement and the intentional masking of this fact is thus closely linked to the rise within a society of hierarchical and statist power. As women are habituated to slavery, hierarchies (from the Greek word ἱεραρχία or hierarkhia, 'rule by the high priest') are established: the path to the enslavement of the other sections of society is thus paved. The enslavement of men

---

1   The concept of 'central civilisation' or 'mainsteam civilisation' is a term from world-systems analysis, coined by David Wilkinson. It means that since its formation through the synthesis of Sumerian and Egyptian civilisation, the central civilisation has absorbed all other existing civilisations and today turned into one single global civilisation.

comes after the enslavement of women. Gender enslavement is different in some ways to class and nation enslavement. Its legitimisation is attained through refined and intense repression combined with lies that play on emotions. Woman's biological difference is used as justification for her enslavement. All the work she does is taken for granted and called unworthy 'woman's work'. Her presence in the public sphere is claimed to be prohibited by religion, morally shameful; progressively, she is secluded from all important social activities. As the dominant power of the political, social and economic activities are taken over by men, the weakness of women becomes even more institutionalised. Thus, the idea of a 'weak sex' becomes a shared belief.

In fact, society treats woman not merely as a biologically separate sex but almost as a separate race, nation or class – the most oppressed race, nation or class: no race, class or nation is subjected to such systematic slavery as housewifisation.

The disappointment experienced due to the failure of any struggle, be it for freedom or equality, or be it a democratic, moral, political or class struggle, bears the imprint of the archetypal struggle for power in a relationship, the one between woman and man. From this relationship stem all forms of relationships that foster inequality, slavery, despotism, fascism and militarism. If we want to construe the true meaning of terms such as *equality, freedom, democracy* and *socialism* that we so often use, we need to analyse and shatter the ancient web of relations that has been woven around women. There is no other way of attaining true equality (with due allowance for diversity), freedom, democracy and morality.

But unambiguously clarifying the status of women is only one aspect of this issue. Far more important is the question of liberation; in other words, the resolution to the problem exceeds the importance of revealing and analysing it. The most promising point in the current chaos of the capitalist system is the (albeit limited) exposure of women's status. During the last quarter of the twentieth century, feminism managed (though not sufficiently) to disclose the truth about women. In times of chaos, the possibility of change for any phenomenon increases in line with the level of progress or clarification available; thus, in such times, small steps taken for freedom may amount to big leaps forward. Women's freedom can emerge as the winner from the current crisis. Whatever has been constructed by the human hand, can be demolished by the human hand. Women's enslavement is neither a law of nature nor is it destiny. What we need is the necessary theory, programme and organisation, and the mechanisms to implement them.

WOMEN'S REVOLUTION: NEOLITHIC ERA

Patriarchy has not always existed. There is strong evidence that in the millennia before the rise of statist civilisation (roughly before 3000 BC) the position of women in society had been very different. Indeed, society was matricentric – it was constructed around women.

Within the Zagros-Taurus system, Mesolithic and subsequently Neolithic society started to develop at the end of the fourth glacial period, around 20,000 years ago. This magnificent society, with its well-developed tools and sophisticated settlement systems, was far more advanced than the preceding clan society. This period constituted a wondrous age in the history of our social nature. Many developments that are still with us can be traced back to this historical stage: the agricultural revolution, the establishment of villages, the roots of trade, and the mother-based family as well as tribes and tribal organisations.

Many methods, tools and equipment we still use today are based on inventions and discoveries most likely made by the women of this era, such as various useful applications of different plants, domestication of animals and cultivation of plants, construction of dwellings, principles of child nutrition, the hoe and hand grinder, perhaps even the ox-cart.

To me, the cult of the mother-goddess in this age symbolises reverence for woman's role in these great advances. I don't see it as deification of an abstract fertility. At the same time, the hierarchy based on the mother-woman is the historic root of the mother-concept, by which all societies still respect and acknowledge the mother as an authority. This authority she demands because the mother is the principal life-element that both gives birth and sustains life through nurturing, even under the most difficult conditions. Indeed, any culture and hierarchy based on this acknowledgement cannot help but revere woman. The true reason for the longevity of the mother-concept is the fact that the mother concretely forms the basis of the social being, the human; it is not due to an abstract ability to give birth.

During the Neolithic period a complete communal social order, so-called 'primordial socialism', was created around woman. This social order saw none of the enforcement practices of the state order; yet it existed for thousands of years. It is this long-lasting order that shaped humanity's collective social consciousness; and it is our endless yearning to regain and immortalise this social order of equality and freedom that led to our construct of paradise.

Primordial socialism, characterised by equality and freedom, was viable because the social morality of the matriarchal order did not allow ownership, which is the main factor behind the widening of social divisions. Division of labour between the sexes, the other issue related to this divide, was not yet based on ownership and power relations. Private relationships inside the group had not yet developed. Food that had been gathered or hunted belonged to all. The children belonged to the clan. No man or woman was the private property of any one person. In all these matters, the community, which was still small and did not have a huge production capacity, had a solid common ideological and material culture. The fundamental principles sustaining society were sharing and solidarity – ownership and force, as life-threatening dangers, would have disrupted this culture.

In contrast to mainstream society, Neolithic society's relationship with nature was maintained, both in terms of ideological and material cultures, through adherence to ecological principles. Nature was regarded as alive and animated, no different from themselves. This awareness of nature fostered a mentality that recognised a multitude of sanctities and divinities in nature. We may gain a better under-standing of the essence of collective life if we acknowledge that it was based on the metaphysics of sanctity and divinity, stemming from reverence for the mother-woman.

What we need to understand is this: why and how was it possible to supersede the matriarchal system of the Neolithic age?

Since the earliest social groupings, there had been tension between woman's gathering and man's hunting, with the result that two different cultural evolutions developed within society.

In the matriarchal society surplus product was, although limited, accumulated. (This was the start of economy – not as a concept but in terms of its essence – and it is here that we find the roots of the different types of economies, such as capitalist and gift economies.) It was woman, the nurturer, who controlled this surplus. But man (quite possibly by developing more successful hunting techniques) bettered his position, achieved a higher status and gathered a retinue around him. The 'wise old man' and shaman, previously not part of the strong man's band, now attached themselves to him and helped to construct the ideology of male dominance. They intended to develop a very systematic movement against women.

In the matriarchal society of the Neolithic age, there were no institutionalised hierarchies; now they were slowly being introduced. The alliance with the shaman and elderly, experienced men was an important development in this regard. The ideological hold the male alliance established over the young men they drew into their circle strengthened their position in the community. What is important is the nature of the power gained by men. Both hunting and defending the clan from external dangers relied on killing and wounding and thus had military characteristics. This was the beginning of the culture of war. In a situation of life and death, one must abide by authority and hierarchy.

Communality is the foundation on which hierarchy and state power are built. Originally, the term 'hierarchy' referred to government by the priests, the authority of the wise elders. Initially, it had a positive function. We may perhaps even view the beneficial hierarchy in a natural society as the prototype of democracy. The mother-woman and the wise elders ensured communal security and the governance of the society; they were necessary and useful, fundamental elements in a society that was not based on accumulation and ownership. Society voluntarily awarded them respect. But when voluntary dependence is transformed into authority, usefulness into self-interest, it always gives way to an uncalled-for instrument of force. The instrument of force disguises itself behind common security and collective production. This constitutes the core of all exploitative and oppressive systems. It is the most sinister creation ever invented; the creation that brought fourth all forms of slavery, all forms of mythology and religion, all systematic annihilation and plunder.

No doubt, there were external reasons for the disintegration of Neolithic society, but the main factor was the sacred state society of the priests. The legends of the initial civilisations in Lower Mesopotamia and along the Nile confirm this. The advanced Neolithic cultures combined with new techniques of artificial irrigation, providing the surplus product required for the establishment of such a society. It was mostly through the newly achieved position and power of man that the urban society which formed around the surplus product was organised in the form of a state.

Urbanisation meant commodification. It resulted in trade. Trade seeped into the veins of Neolithic society in the form of colonies. Commodification, exchange value and ownership grew exponentially, thus accelerating the disintegration of Neolithic society.

THE FIRST MAJOR SEXUAL RUPTURE

In the vein of the *revolution/counter-revolution* scheme of historical materialism, I suggest that we term the remarkable turning points in the history of the relationship between the sexes *sexual rupture*. History has seen two of these ruptures and, I predict, will see another in the future.

In the social ages preceding civilisation, the organised force of the 'strong man' existed for the sole purposes of trapping animals and defence against outside danger. It is this organised force that coveted the family-clan unit that the woman had established as a product of her emotional labour. The takeover of the family-clan constituted the first serious organisation of violence. What was usurped in the process was woman herself, her children and kin, and all their material and moral cultural accumulation. It was the plunder of the initial economy, the home economy. The organised force of proto-priest (shaman), experienced elder and strong man allied to compose the initial and longest enduring patriarchal hierarchic power, that of holy governance. This can be seen in all societies that are at a similar stage: until the class, city and state stage, this hierarchy is dominant in social and economic life.

In Sumerian society, although the balance gradually turned against the woman, the two sexes were still more or less equal until the second millennium BC. The many temples for goddesses and the mythological texts from this period indicate that between 4,000 and 2,000 BC the influence of the woman-mother culture on the Sumerians, who formed the centre of civilisation, was on par with that of the man. As yet, no culture of shame had developed around the woman.

So, we see here the start of a new culture that develops its superiority over the mother-woman cult. The development of this authority and hierarchy before the start of class-based society constitutes one of the most important turning points in history. This culture is qualitatively different from the mother-woman culture. Gathering, and later cultivation – the predominant elements of the mother-woman culture – are peaceful activities that do not require warfare. Hunting, which is predominantly taken up by man, rests on war culture and harsh authority.

It is understandable that the strong man, whose essential role was hunting, coveted the accumulation of the matriarchal order. Establishing his dominance would yield many advantages. Organisation of the power he gained through hunting now gave him the opportunity to rule and to establish the first social hierarchy. This development constituted the first usage of analytical intelligence with malignant intentions; subsequently, it became systemic. Furthermore, the transition from sacred mother cult to sacred father cult enabled analytical intelligence to mask itself behind sanctity.

Thus, the origin of our serious social problems is to be found in patriarchal societies that became cult-like – that is, religionised – around the strong man. With the enslavement of women, the ground was prepared for the enslavement of not only children but also of men. As man gained experience in accumulating values through the use of slave labour (especially accumulating surplus product), his control over and domination of these slaves grew. Power and authority became increasingly important. The collaboration between the strong man, experienced elder and shaman to form a privileged sector, resulted in a power centre that was difficult to resist. In this centre, analytical intelligence developed an extraordinary mythological narrative in order to rule the minds of the populace. In the mythological world composed for Sumerian society (and passed down through the ages with some adaptations), man is exalted to the point that he is deified as creator of heaven and earth. While woman's divinity and sacredness is first demeaned and then erased, the idea of man as ruler and absolute power is imprinted on society. Thus, through an enormous network of mythological narratives, every aspect of culture is cloaked in the relationship of ruler and ruled, creator and created. Society is beguiled into internalising this mythological world and gradually it becomes the preferred version. Then it is turned into religion, a religion into which the concept of a strict distinction between people is built. For instance, the class division of society is reflected in the story of Adam and Eve's expulsion from paradise and condemnation to servitude. This legend endows the Sumerian ruler-gods with creative power; their subjects are recreated as servants.

Sumerian mythology knew the story of creation out of the rib of an anthropomorphic god – only, it was the goddess Ninhursag who carried out the act of creation in order to save the life of the male god Enki. Over time, the narrative was changed to benefit the man. The repetitive elements of rivalry and creativity in the myths of Enki and Ninhursag-Inanna had the twofold function of, on the one hand, demeaning woman and diminishing the importance of her past creativity and, on the other hand, symbolising the forming of a human that is but a slave and a servant. (I believe that this last conception of the Sumerian priests has played a role in all subsequent god–servant dilemmas. To determine the truth of this is vital; nevertheless, religious literature either refrains from doing so or rejects the notion out of hand. Is this because theologians feel the need to disguise the truth and hence their interests in the matter?)

The divine identities designed in Sumerian society are the reflections of a new approach to nature and of new societal powers; more than that, they are almost *deployed* for the purpose of conditioning the mind anew. Hand in hand with the decreasing influence of the natural dimension, the societal dimension gains importance; women's influence gradually decreases; and there are striking developments in the matter of identifying the human being as subject, as servant. While growing political power in society results in the prominence of some of the gods, it also results in the loss of some identities and a significant change in the form of others. Thus, the absolute power of the monarch during the Babylonian era is reflected in the rise of the god Marduk. This last phase of Sumerian mythology indicates that the threshold of the birth of monotheistic religions had been reached.

In an order like this, where men owned the children, the father would want to have as many children as possible (especially male children), for attainment of power. Command of the children enabled him to seize the mother-woman's accumulation: the ownership system was created. Alongside the priest-state's collective ownership, the private ownership of the dynasty was established. Private ownership too necessitated the establishment of fatherhood: fatherhood rights were required so that the inheritance could be passed on (mainly) to the male children.

From 2000 BC onwards, this culture became widespread. Woman's social status was radically altered. Patriarchal society had gained the strength to make its rule legendary. While the world of the male is exalted and hero-worshipped, everything female is belittled, demeaned and vilified.

So radical was this sexual rupture, that it resulted in the most significant change in social life that history has ever seen. This change concerning woman's value within Middle Eastern culture, we can call the first major sexual rupture or counter-revolution. I call it a counter-revolution because it has contributed nothing to the positive development of society. On the contrary, it has led to an extraordinary poverty of life by bringing about patriarchy's stiff domination of society and the exclusion of women. This tear in Middle Eastern civilisation is arguably the first step in its pro-gressively deteriorating situation, as the negative consequences of this rupture just keep on multiplying as time goes on. Instead of a dual-voiced society, it produced a single-voiced, male society. A transition was made to a one-dimensional, extremely masculine social culture. The emotional intelligence of woman that created wonders, that was humane and committed to nature and life, was lost. In its place was born the cursed analytical intelligence of a cruel culture that surrendered itself to dogmatism and detached itself from nature; that considers war to be the most exalted virtue and enjoys the shedding of human blood; that sees the arbitrary treatment of woman and the enslavement of man as its right. *This* intelligence is the antitype of the egalitarian intelligence of woman that is focused on humanitarian production and animate nature.

The mother has become the ancient goddess; she now sits in her home, an obedient and chaste woman. Far from being equal to the gods, she cannot make her voice heard or reveal her face. Slowly, she is wrapped in veils, and becomes a captive within the harem of the strong man.

The depth of woman's enslavement in Arabia (intensified in the Abrahamic tradition by Moses) is linked to this historical development.

HOW PATRIARCHAL AUTHORITY
BECAME DEEP-ROOTED

A hierarchical and authoritarian structure is essential for a patriarchal society. Allying authoritarian administration with the shaman's sacred authority resulted in the concept of hierarchy. The institution of authority would gradually gain prominence in society, and as class distinctions intensified it would transform into state authority. At the time, hierarchical authority was personal, not yet institutionalised, and thus did not have as much dominance over society as in the institutionalised state. Compliance to it was partly voluntary, commitment determined by society's interests.

However, the process that was set in motion was conducive to the birth of the hierarchical state. The primordial communal system resisted this process for a long time. Respect and commitment to the authority of the alliance was shown only if they shared their accumulated products with other members of society. In fact, accumulation of surplus product was seen as wrong; the person who commanded the most respect was the one who distributed his or her accumulation. (The revered tradition of generosity, which is still widespread in clan societies, has its roots in this powerful historical tradition.) From the very beginning, the community saw accumulation of surplus product as the most serious threat to itself, and based its morality and religion on resisting this threat. But, eventually, man's accumulation culture and hierarchical authority did defeat that of woman. We must be very clear that this victory was not an unavoidable, historical necessity. There is no law that states that a natural society must necessarily develop into a hierarchical and subsequently statist society. There may be a propensity towards such a development, but equating such a propensity with an inevitable, incessant process that has to run its full course would be an erroneous assumption. Viewing the existence of classes as fate has become nothing but an unintended tool for class ideologists.

After this defeat, damaging tears appeared in woman's communal society. The process of transforming into hierarchical society was not an easy one. This was the transition phase between primitive communal society and the state. Eventually hierarchical society either had to disintegrate or result in statehood. Although it did play some positive role in the development of society, its form of socialisation, the alliance between the male powers, provided the strength for hierarchical patriarchy to develop into statehood. It was really the hierarchical and patriarchal society that subjugated women, youth and members of other ethnicities; it was done before the development of the state. The most important point is *how* this subjugation was accomplished. The authority to do this was not attained through laws, but through the new morals that were based on worldly needs instead of sacredness.

While there is a development towards the religious concept of an abstract and single god that reflects the values of the patriarchal society, the matriarchal authority of natural society with its myriad goddesses resists. In the matriarchal order, the essential rules are to labour, produce and provide in order to keep people alive. While patriarchal morality legitimises accumulation and paves the way for ownership, the morality of communal society condemns accumulation of surplus as the source of all wrong-doing, and encourages its distribution. The internal harmony in society gradually deteriorates and tension increases.

The solution to this conflict would be either returning to the old matriarchal values, or escalating patriarchal power inside and outside the community. To the patriarchal faction there was only one choice. The foundations for a violent, war-like society based on oppression and exploitation were established.

Through this process of conflict the state phase, the phase of institutionalised authority based on permanent force, began.

Without an analysis of woman's status in the hierarchical system and the conditions under which she was enslaved, neither the state nor the class-based system that it rests upon can be understood. Woman is not targeted as the female gender, but as the founder of the matriarchal society. Without a thorough analysis of woman's enslavement and establishing the conditions for overcoming it, no other slavery can be analysed or overcome. Without these analyses, fundamental mistakes cannot be avoided.

ALL SLAVERY IS BASED ON HOUSEWIFISATION

Ever since the hierarchical order's enormous leap forward, sexism has been the basic ideology of power. It is closely linked to class division and the wielding of power. Woman's authority is not based on surplus product; on the contrary, it stems from fertility and productivity, and strengthens social existence. Strongly influenced by emotional intelligence, she is tightly bound to communal existence. The fact that woman does not have a visible place in the power wars based on surplus product is due to this position of hers in social existence.

We need to point out a characteristic that has become institutionalised within civilisational societies, namely society's being prone to power relations. Just as housewifisation was needed to recreate woman, society needed to be prepared in order for power to secure its own existence. Housewifisation is the oldest form of slavery. The strong man and his entourage defeated the mother-woman and all aspects of her cult through long and comprehensive struggles. Housewifisation became institutionalised when the sexist society became dominant. Gender discrimination is not a notion restricted to the power relations between woman and man. It defines the power relations that have been spread to all social levels. It is indicative of the state power that has reached its maximum capacity with modernity.

Gender discrimination has had a twofold destructive effect on society. First, it has opened society to slavery; second, all other forms of enslavement have been implemented on the basis of housewifisation. Housewifisation does not only aim to recreate an individual as a sex object; it is not a result of a biological characteristic. Housewifisation is an intrinsically social process and targets the whole of society. Slavery, subjugation, subjection to insults, weeping, habitual lying, unassertiveness and flaunting oneself are all recognised aspects of housewifisation and must be rejected by the freedom-morality. It is the foundation of a degraded society and the true foundation of slavery. It is the institutional foundation upon which the oldest and all subsequent types of slavery and immorality were implemented. Civilisational society reflects this foundation in all social categories. If the system is to function, society in its entirety must be subjected to housewifisation. Power is synonymous with masculinity. Thus, society's subjection to housewifisation is inevitable, because power does not recognise the principles of freedom and equality. If it did, it could not exist. Power and sexism in society share the same essence.

Another important point we have to mention is dependence and oppression of the youth, established by the experienced elderly man in a hierarchical society. While experience strengthens the elderly man, age renders him weak and powerless. This compels the elderly to enlist the youth, which is done by winning their minds. Patriarchy is strengthened tremendously by these means. The physical power of the youth enables them to do whatever they please. This dependency of the youth has been continuously perpetuated and deepened. Superiority of experience and ideology cannot easily be broken. The youth (and even the children) are subjugated to the same strategies and tactics, ideological and political propaganda, and oppressive systems as the woman – adolescence, like femininity, is not a physical but a social fact.

This must be clearly understood: it is not coincidence that the first powerful authority to be established was authority over woman. Woman represents the power of the organic, natural and egalitarian society which had not experienced oppressive and exploitative relations. Patriarchy could not have been victorious if she was not defeated; moreover, the transition to the institution of the state could not have been made. Breaking the power of the mother-woman thus was of strategic significance. No wonder that it was such an arduous process.

Without analysing the process through which woman was socially overcome, one cannot properly understand the fundamental characteristics of the consequent male-dominated social culture.

Even awareness of the societal establishment of masculinity will be impossible. Without understanding how masculinity was socially formed, one cannot analyse the institution of state and therefore will not be able to accurately define the war and power culture related to statehood. I stress this issue because we need to expose the macabre godlike personalities that developed as a result of all later class divisions, and all the different types of exploitation and murder they have done. The social subjugation of woman was the vilest counter-revolution ever carried out.

Power has reached its full capacity in the form of the nation-state. It derives its strength mainly from the sexism it spreads and intensifies by the integration of women into the labour force as well as through nationalism and militarism. Sexism, just as nationalism, is an ideology through which power is generated and nation-states are built. Sexism is not a function of biological differences. To the dominant male, the female is an object to be used for the realisation of his ambitions. In the same vein, when the housewifisation of woman was done, he started the process of turning men into slaves; subsequently the two forms of slavery became intertwined.

In short, the campaigns for excluding women and for manufacturing reverence for the conquering, warrior male authority structure were tightly interwoven. The state as an institution was invented by males and wars of plunder and pillage were almost its sole mode of production. Woman's societal influence, based on production, was replaced by man's societal influence, based on war and pillage. There is a close link between woman's captivity and the warrior societal culture. War does not produce, it seizes and plunders. Although force can be decisive for social progress under certain unique conditions (e.g. the way to freedom is won through resistance to occupation, invasion and colonialism), but more often than not it is destructive and negative.

The culture of violence that has become internalised within society is fed by war. The sword of war wielded in state warfare and the hand of the man within the family, which are both symbols of hegemony. The entire class-based society, from its upper layers to its lower layers, is clamped between the sword and the hand.

This is something that I have always tried to understand: how is it possible that the power held by the woman fell into the hands of the man, who is not very productive and creative. The answer lies of course in the role that force has played. When the economy was taken from the woman, atrocious captivity was inevitable.

THE SECOND MAJOR SEXUAL RUPTURE

Millennia after the establishment of patriarchy (what I call the 'first major sexual rupture') women were once again dealt a blow from which they are still struggling to recover. I am referring to the intensification of patriarchy through the monotheistic religions.

The mentality of rejecting the natural society deepened in the feudal social system. Religious and philosophical thought constituted the new society's dominant mentality. In the same way that Sumerian society had synthesised the values of Neolithic society into its own new system, feudal society synthesised the moral values of the oppressed classes from the old system and the resisting ethnic groups from the remote areas into its own internal structures. The development of polytheism into monotheism played an important part in this process.

The mythological features of this mindset were renewed with religious and philosophical concepts. The rising power of the empire was reflected in the multitude of powerless gods that evolved into an omnipotent, universal god.

The culture concerning women that was developed by the monotheistic religions resulted in the second major sexual rupture. Where the rupture of the mythological period was a cultural requirement, the rupture of the monotheistic period was 'the law as God commands'. Treating women as inferior now became the sacred command of God. The superiority of man in the new religion is illustrated by the relationship between the prophet Abraham and the women Sarah and Hagar. Patriarchy was at that point well established. The institution of concubinage was formed; polygamy approved. As indicated by the fierce relationship between the prophet Moses and his sister Mariam, woman's share in the cultural heritage was eradicated. The society of the prophet Moses was a total male society in which women were not given any task. *This* is what the fight with Mariam was about.

In the period of the Hebrew kingdom that rose just before the end of the first millennium BC, we see, with David and Solomon, the transition to a culture of extensive housewifisation. Woman under the dual domination of the patriarchal culture and the religious state culture plays no public role. The best woman is the one who conforms most to her man or patriarchy. Religion becomes a tool to slander woman. Primarily, she – Eve – was the first sinful woman who seduced Adam, resulting in his expulsion from paradise. Lilith does not subjugate herself to Adam's god (a patriarchal figure) and befriends the chief of the evil spirits (a human figure who rejects being a servant and does not obey Adam). Indeed, the Sumerian claim that woman was created from man's rib was included in the Bible. As pointed out earlier, this is a complete reversal of the original narrative – from women being the creator to being the created. Women are hardly mentioned as prophets in the religious traditions. Woman's sexuality is seen as the most wretched evil and has continuously been vilified and besmirched. Woman, who still had an honoured place in Sumerian and Egyptian societies, now became a figure of disgrace, sin and seduction.

With the arrival of the period of the prophet Jesus, came the figure of Mother Mary. Although she is the mother of the Son of God, there is no trace left of her former goddess-ness. An extremely quiet, weeping mother (without the title of goddess!) has replaced the mother-goddess. The fall continues. It is quite ironic that a mere woman is impregnated by God. In fact, the trinity of Father, Son and Holy Spirit represents the synthesis of polytheistic religions and monotheistic religion. While Mary too should have been considered a god, she is seen as merely a tool of the Holy Spirit. This indicates that divinity has become exclusively male. In the Sumerian and

Egyptian periods, gods and goddesses were almost equal. Even during the Babylonian era the voice of the mother-goddess was still heard clearly and loudly.

Woman no longer had any social role bar being the woman of her house. Her primary duty was looking after her male children, the 'son-gods', whose value had increased greatly since the mythological period. The public sphere was closed off to her. Christianity's praxis of saintly virgin women was in fact a retreat into seclusion in order to find salvation from sins. At least this saintly, cloistered life offered some deliverance from sexism and condemnation. There are good and strong material and spiritual reasons for choosing life in a cloister above the hell-like life at home. We can almost call this institution the first poor women's party. Monogamy, which had been well established in Judaism, was taken over by Christianity and sanctified. This praxis has an important place in the history of European civilisation. A negative aspect is that women are treated as sexual objects in European civilisation because Catholics are not allowed to divorce.

With the coming of the prophet Muhammad and Islam, the status of women in the patriarchal culture of the desert tribes improved somewhat. But in its essence, Islam based itself on the Abrahamic culture; women had the same status during the period of the prophet Muhammad as they had in the period of David and Solomon. As then, multiple marriages for political reasons and numerous concubines were legitimate. Although in Islam marriage is restricted to four women, in essence it is unchanged because the owning of harems and concubines became institutionalised.

Both the Christian and Muslim cultures have become stagnant in terms of overcoming sexist society. The policies of Christianity towards women and sexuality in general are what lie behind the crisis of modernist monogamous life. This is the reality behind the crisis of sexist culture in Western society.

This can also not be solved by celibacy as it is demanded from priests and nuns. The Islamic solution, giving priority to male sexual fulfilment with many women in the position of wife and concubine, has been just as unsuccessful. In essence, the harem is but a privatised brothel for the sole use of the privileged individual. The sexist social practices of the harem and polygamy have had a deterministic role in Middle Eastern society falling behind Western society. While the restraining of sexuality by Christianity is a factor that has led to modernity, encouraging excessive sexual fulfilment is a factor that has led to Islam regressing to a state worse than the old desert tribal society, and to it being surpassed by the society of Western modernity.

The effect of sexism on societal development is far bigger than we assume. When analysing the growing gap between Eastern and Western societal development, we should focus on the role of sexism. Islam's perception of sexism has produced far more negative results than Western civilisation in terms of the profound enslavement of woman and male dominance.

Societal servitude is not just a class phenomenon. There is an order of subjugation which is more deeply hidden than the slave-owning system itself. The softening of this truth contributes to the deepening of the system. The fundamental paradigm of society is a system of servitude which has no beginning and no end.

FAMILY, DYNASTY AND STATE

I have mentioned the intense relationship between the power relations within the patriarchal family and the state. This deserves a closer look.

The cornerstones of dynastic ideology are the patriarchal family, fatherhood and having many male children. This can be traced back to the understanding of political power in the patriarchal system. While the priest established his power through his so-called ability to give and interpret meaning, the strong man established his leadership through the use of political power. Political power can be understood as the use of force when leadership is not adhered to. On the other hand, the power of priest rests on 'God's wrath' when not abided; it is spiritual power and thus has a stimulating effect.

The true source of political power is the military entourage of the strong man.

Dynasty, as ideology and in practice, developed as a result of turning this system upside down. Within the patriarchal order, patriarchal governance became deep-rooted as a consequence of the alliance between the 'experienced old man', the 'strong man' with his military entourage and the shaman who, as the sacred leader, was the forerunner of the priest.

The dynastic system should be understood as an integrated whole, where ideology and structure cannot be separated. It developed from within the tribal system but established itself as the upper-class administrative family nucleus, thereby denying the tribal system. It has a very strict hierarchy. It is a proto-ruling class, the prototype of power and state. It depends on man and male children; owning many is important in order to have power. A consequence of this has been polygamy, the harem and the concubine system. Creation of power and the state is the dynasty's first priority. More importantly, dynasty was the very first institution that ensured its own clan and tribes, as well as other tribal systems, became accustomed to class division and slavery. In Middle Eastern civilisation it has become so deep-rooted that there is almost no power or state that is not a dynasty. Because it constitutes a training ground for power and state, it is continually perpetuated and very difficult to overcome.

Every man in the family perceives himself to be the owner of a small kingdom. This dynastic ideology is effectively reason why family is such an important issue. The greater the number of women and children that belong to the family, the more security and dignity the man attains. It is also important to analyse the current family as an ideological institution. If we are to eliminate woman and family from the civilisational system, its power and state, there will be little left to constitute the order. But the price of this will be the painful, poverty-stricken, degraded and defeated existence of woman under a never-ending, low-intensity state of warfare. The male monopoly that has been maintained over the life and world of woman throughout history is not unlike the monopoly chain that capital maintains over society. More importantly, it is the oldest powerful monopoly. We might draw more realistic conclusions if we evaluate woman's existence as the oldest colonial phenomenon. It may be more accurate to call women the oldest colonised people who have never become a nation.

Family, in this social context, developed as man's small state. The family as an institution has been continuously perfected throughout the history of civilisation, solely because of the reinforcement it provides to power and state apparatus. First, family is turned into a stem cell of state society by giving power to the family in the person of the male. Second, woman's unlimited and unpaid labour is secured. Third, she raises children in order to meet population needs. Fourth, as a role model she disseminates slavery and immorality to the whole society. Family, thus constituted, is the institution where dynastic ideology becomes functional.

The most important problem for freedom in a social context is thus family and marriage. When the woman marries, she is in fact enslaved. It is impossible to imagine another institution that enslaves like marriage. The most profound slaveries are established by the institution of marriage, slaveries that become more entrenched within the family. This is not a general reference to sharing life or partner relationships that can be meaningful depending on one's perception of freedom and equality. What is under discussion is the ingrained, classical marriage and family. Absolute ownership of woman means her withdrawal from all political, intellectual, social and economic arenas; this cannot be easily recovered. Thus, there is a need to radically review family and marriage and develop common guidelines aimed at democracy, freedom and gender equality. Marriages or relationships that arise from individual, sexual needs and traditional family concepts can cause some of the most dangerous deviations on the way to a free life. Our need is not for these associations but for attaining gender equality and democracy throughout society and for the will to shape a suitable and common life. This can only be done by analysing the mentality and political environment that breed such destructive associations.

The dynastic and family culture that remains so powerful in today's Middle Eastern society is one of the main sources of its problems, because it has given rise to an excessive population, with the power and ambitions to share in the state's power. The degradation of women, inequality, children not being educated, family brawls and problems of honour are all related to the family issue. It is as if a small model of the problems integral to power and state are established within the family. Thus, it is essential to analyse the family in order to analyse power, state, class and society.

State and power centres gave the father-man within the family a copy of their own authority and had them play that role. Thus, the family became the most important tool for legitimising monopolies. It became the fountainhead of slaves, serfs, labourers, soldiers and providers of all other services required by the ruling and capitalist rings. That is why they set such importance in family, why they sanctified it. Although woman's labour is the most important source of profit for the capitalist rings, they concealed this by putting additional burdens on the family. Family has been turned into the insurance of the system and thus it will inevitably be perpetuated.

Critique of family is vital. Remnants from past patriarchal and state societies and patterns from modern Western civilisation have not created a synthesis but an impasse in the Middle East. The bottleneck created within the family is even more tangled than the one within the state. If the family continues to maintain its strength in contrast to other, faster dissolving social bonds, this is because it is the only available social shelter. We should *not* discount family. If soundly analysed, family can become the mainstay of democratic society. Not only the woman but the whole family should be analysed as the stem cell of power; if not, we will leave the ideal and the implementation of democratic civilisation without its most important element.

Family is not a social institution that should be overthrown. But it should be transformed. The claim of ownership over women and children, handed down from the hierarchy, should be abandoned. Capital (in all its forms) and power relations should have no part in the relationship of couples. The breeding of children as motivation for sustaining this institution should be abolished. The ideal approach to male–female association is one that is based on the freedom philosophy, devoted to moral and political society. Within this framework, the transformed family will be the most robust assurance of democratic civilisation and one of the fundamental relationships within that order. Natural companionship is more important than official partnership. Partners should always accept the other's right to live alone. One cannot act in a slavish or reckless manner in relationships.

Clearly, the family will experience its most meaningful transformation during democratic civilisation. If woman, who has been stripped of much of her strength and respect, does not regain this, meaningful family unions cannot be developed. There can be no respect for a family that is established on ignorance. In the construction of democratic civilisation, the role of the family is vital.

WOMEN'S SITUATION IN KURDISH SOCIETY

Thus far, I have described some general characteristics of sexist society. Let me conclude this analysis with some remarks on the specific conditions of Kurdish women.

The transition from the Sumerian to the Hittite civilisation (during the second millennium BC) pushed the proto-Kurds to strengthen their tribal existence. Because a premature statehood would have caused their elimination, they seemed to have preferred a semi-nomadic, semi-guerrilla lifestyle. As more and more states were established around them, they felt an increasing need to strengthen their tribal structures. Kurdish tribalism resembled the lifestyle of a guerrilla group. When we take a closer look at the family within the tribal organisation, we see the prominence of matriarchy and freedom. Women were quite influential and free. The alertness, strength and courage of present-day Kurdish women originates from this very old historical tradition. However, a negative aspect of tribal life is that opportunities to make the transition to a more advanced society are restricted.

It is not a coincidence that among the peoples of the Middle East the Kurds have the best-developed sense of freedom. We see this in their historical development. The prolonged absence of the ruling and exploitative classes and their inability to generate any positive value for their community, plus the fact that throughout their history Kurds have had to fight nature and foreign incursions, have all contributed to the development of this characteristic. The fact that women in Kurdish society are more prominent than in other Middle Eastern societies is due to this historical reality.

However, the present situation of women in Kurdish society needs to be analysed thoroughly. The situation of women throughout the world is bad, but that of Kurdish women is nothing but terrible slavery and is unique in many respects. In fact, the situation of both women and children are appalling.

Although in Kurdistan family is considered sacred, it has been crushed – especially as a result of a lack of freedom, economic inability, lack of education and health problems. The phenomenon of so-called honour killings is the symbolic revenge for what has happened to society in general. Women are made to pay for the obliteration of society's honour. Loss of masculinity is taken out on women. Except for women's honour, the Kurdish male, who has lost both moral and political strength, has no other area left to prove his power or powerlessness.

Under the present circumstances, it may be possible to resolve the family crisis if there is a general democratisation of society. Education and broadcasting in the mother tongue can partially eliminate identity impairment. Marriage, the relations between husband, wife and children, has not even surpassed that of the old feudal relationships when capitalism mercilessly besieged them and turned their life into a complete prison.

In its freedom struggle for the Kurdish people, the PKK did not only fight against the crippling effects of colonialism; above all, it struggled against internal feudalism in order to change the status of women and end the enslavement of society in general. Women were attracted to the struggle in great numbers – not only to resist colonialism, but also to end internal feudalism and to demand freedom. Since the 1980s, this has caused Kurdish women, whether within or outside the organisation, to organise themselves as a movement and to take and implement decisions that concern not only them as women but also society in general. I have tried to support them in any way I can, both theoretically and in practice.

CAPITALISM

A realistic definition of capitalism should not present it as a constant, created and characterised by unicentral thought and action. It is, in essence, the result of the actions of opportunist individuals and groups who established themselves into openings and cracks within society as the potential for surplus product developed; these actions became systematised as they nibbled away at the social surplus.

These individuals and groups never number more than 1 or 2 per cent of society. Their strength is in their opportunism and organisational skills. Their victory relies not only on their organisational skills but also on their control of the required objects and fluctuation of prices at the point where supply and demand intersect. If official social forces do not suppress them – if, instead, these forces borrow from their profiteering, giving their continuous support in return – then these groups who exist on the margins of all societies may legitimise themselves as the new masters of society. Throughout the history of civilisation, especially in Middle Eastern societies, these marginal groups of broker-profiteers have always existed. But because of society's hatred of them, they could never find the courage to come into the daylight from the fissures they resided in. Not even the most despotic administrators had the courage to legitimise these groups. They were not just scorned, but seen as the most dangerous corruptive power; their ethics were considered the root of all evil. And indeed, the unsurpassed wave of wars, plunders, massacres and exploitation originating from Western Europe over the last 400 years is largely a result of the capitalist system's hegemony. (But then, the biggest counter-struggle also took place in Western Europe, hence it cannot be considered a total loss for humanity.)

Capitalism and the nation-state represent the dominant male in its most institutionalised form. Capitalist society is the continuation and culmination of all the old exploitative societies. It is continuous warfare against society and woman. To put it succinctly, capitalism and the nation-state are the monopolism of the tyrannical and exploitative male.

Breaking down this monopolism will perhaps be more difficult than breaking down the atom. A main objective of capitalist modernity's ideological hegemony is to obliterate the historic and social facts concerning its conception and its essence. This is because the capitalist economic and societal form is not a social and historical necessity; it is a construct, forged through a complex process. Religion and philosophy have been transformed into nationalism, the divinity of the nation-state. The ultimate goal of its ideological warfare is to ensure its monopoly on thought. Its main weapons to accomplish this are religionism, gender discrimination and scientism as a positivist religion. Without ideological hegemony, with political and military oppression alone, maintaining modernity will be impossible. While capitalism uses religionism to control society's cognisance, it uses nationalism to control classes and citizenship, a phenomenon that has risen around capitalism. The objective of gender discrimination is to deny women any hope of change. The most effective way for sexist ideology to function is by entrapping the male in power relations and by rendering woman impotent through constant rape. Through positivist scientism, capitalism neutralises the academic world and the youth. It convinces them that they have no choice but to integrate with the system, and in return for concessions this integration is assured.

As with all oppressive and exploitative social systems, capitalism could not rise without establishing a state. Whereas the dogmatism of the feudal system had a religious character, that of the archaic slave-owning society had a mythological character. One god was embodied in the king and dynasty; but today God is presented as the invisible power in the state's noble existence.

When capitalism saw the opportunity to become a system, it started off by eliminating all societies based on the mother-woman culture. During early modernity, the strength of female sociality that was still trying to maintain itself was burnt on the stake of the witch-hunter. In order to establish its hegemony over woman through her profound enslavement, these burnings were very useful tools. Woman is at the service of the system today partly because of the widespread burning of women at the onset of capitalism. The embedded fear of the stake has put women in Europe under the total servitude of men.

After eliminating women, the system mercilessly demolished agrarian and village society. As long as the communal democratic character of society stands, capitalism cannot attain maximum power and profits. Thus, this kind of sociality was inevitably targeted. In this way, the complete entrapment of the oldest slave, woman, became the model for all other enslaved lives – that of children and men.

Political and military power play an important role in maintaining the capitalist system's hegemony. But what is crucial is to possess and subsequently to paralyse society via the culture industry. The mentality of communities under the influence of the system has weakened and its members have become gullible. Many philosophers claim that society has been turned into a society of the spectacle, similar to a zoo. The sex, sports, arts and culture industries, in combination and in sequence, bombard emotional and analytic intelligence incessantly by means of a diverse spread of advertisements. As a result, both emotional and analytical intelligence have become completely dysfunctional; the conquering of society's mentality is thus complete.

What is of grave concern is society's voluntary acceptance of its captivity by the combined cultural and sex industries, and moreover, perceiving this as a burst of freedom! This is the strongest base and tool of legitimisation the rulers have. Capitalism can only reach the empire phase with the aid of the culture industry. Therefore, the struggle against cultural hegemony requires the most difficult struggle of all: mental struggle. Until we can develop and organise the essence and form of a counter-struggle against the cultural war waged by the system through its invasions, assimilation and industrialisation, not a single struggle for freedom, equality and democracy has a chance of succeeding.

Capitalist modernity is a system based on the denial of love. Its denial of society, unrestrained individualism, gender discrimination in all areas, deification of money, substitution of God with the nation-state and turning woman into an automaton that receives no or little wages, mean that there are no material grounds for love either.

ECONOMY

Economy has been turned into subject matter that ordinary people are not supposed to understand. It has intentionally been made complicated so that the plain reality can be disguised. It is the third force, after ideology and violence, through which women, and subsequently the entire society, was entrapped and forced to accept dependence. *Economy* literally means 'householding', originally the women's domain, along with other fundamental sections of society which I will discuss later.

In the woman's order, there was accumulation too, but this was not for the merchant or the market. It was for the family. This is what humanitarian and real economy is. Accumulation was prevented from becoming a danger by widespread use of the gift culture. Gift culture is an important form of economic activity. It is also compatible with the rhythm of human development.

As woman was ousted generally from the history of civilisation but specifically from capitalist modernity, big men had the opportunity to distort the functioning of economy and thus turning it into a mass of problems. This was done by people with no organic link to the economy because of their excessive lust for profit and power.

They thus placed all economic forces, especially woman, under their own control. The result is that the forces of power and state have grown excessively, like a tumour on society, to the extent where it can no longer be sustained or maintained.

The economic problem actually begins as the woman is ousted from the economy. In essence, economy is everything that has to do with nourishment. It may seem peculiar, but I believe that woman is still the real creator of economy, despite all attempts to overrun and colonise her. A thorough analysis of the economy will show that woman is the most fundamental force of economy. Indeed, this is clear when we consider her role in the agricultural revolution, and how she gathered plants for millions of years. Today, she not only works inside the home but in many areas of economic life; she is the one that keeps on turning the wheel. After woman, those who can be classified as slaves, serfs and workers would be second in line to the claim of being creators of economy. They have been kept under control continuously and cruelly so that the civilisational powers can seize their surplus product and value. Third in line are all the artisans, small merchant-shopkeepers and small landowner-farmers who are, admittedly, a little freer. To this category we can add the artists, architects, engineers, doctors and all other self-employed people. This just about completes the picture of those who create and constitute the economy.

The most brutal period for woman was when she was ousted from the economy during the process of capitalist civilisation. This leaves the woman destitute of economy, which has become the most striking and profound social paradox. The entire female population has been left 'unemployed'. Although housework can be the most arduous work, it is seen as valueless. Although childbirth and child rearing are the most exacting tasks of all, they are not always regarded as valuable but often as a mere nuisance. On top of being an unemployed childbearing and child raising machine that is inexpensive to purchase and can be run cost-free, woman can be used as scapegoat, carrying the guilt for all that is wrong. Throughout the history of civilisation, she has been placed on the ground floor of society where she does her unpaid housework, raises the children and keeps the family together; duties that form the actual basis of capitalist accumulation. Indeed, no other society has had the power to develop and systemise the exploitation of woman to the degree that capitalism has.

During the capitalist period woman has been a target of inequality, with no freedom and no democracy, not only at the ground level but at all levels. Moreover, the power of the sexist society has been implemented with such intensity and so deeply that woman has been turned into object *and* subject of the sex industry. The male-dominant society has reached its peak in capitalist civilisation.

Woman and economy are interwoven components. Because she generates economy according to fundamental needs only, a woman-driven economy never experiences depression; it never causes environmental pollution; and it never poses a threat to the climate. When we cease to produce for profit, we will have achieved the liberation of the world. This in turn will be the liberation of humanity and life itself.

KILLING THE DOMINANT MALE: INSTITUTING THE THIRD MAJOR SEXUAL RUPTURE AGAINST THE DOMINANT MALE

Although male dominance is well institutionalised, men too are enslaved. The system is in fact reproducing itself in the individual male and female and their relationship. Therefore, if we want to defeat the system, we need a radical, new approach towards woman, man and their relationship.

History, in a sense, is the history of the dominant male who gained power with the rise of classed society. The ruling class character is formed concurrently with the dominant male character. Again, rule is validated through mythological lies and divine punishment. Beneath these masks lies the reality of bare force and coarse exploitation. In the name of honour, man seized the position and rights of woman in the most insidious, traitorous and despotic manner. The fact that, throughout history, woman was left bereft of her identity and character – the eternal captive – at the hands of man, has caused considerably more damage than class division has. The captivity of woman is a measure of society's general enslavement and decline; it is also a measure of its lies, theft and tyranny. The dominant male character of society has to date not even allowed for scientific analysis of the phenomenon of woman.

The fundamental question is why is man so jealous, dominant and villainous where woman is concerned; why does he continue to play the rapist? Undoubtedly, rape and domination are phenomena related to social exploitation; they reflect society's rape by hierarchy, patriarchy and power. If we look a little deeper, we will see that these acts also express a betrayal of life. Woman's multifaceted devotion to life may clarify man's societal sexist stand. Societal sexism means the loss of wealth of life under the blinding and exhausting influence of sexism and the consequent rise of anger, rape and a dominating stance.

This is why it is important to place on the agenda the problem of man, which is far more serious than the issue of woman. It is probably more difficult to analyse the concepts of domination and power, concepts related to man. It is not woman but man that is not willing to transform. He fears that abandoning the role of the dominant male figure would leave him in the position of the monarch who has lost his state. He should be made aware that this most hollow form of domination leaves him bereft of freedom as well and, even worse, it forecloses reform.

In order to lead a meaningful life, we need to define woman and her role in societal life. This should not be a statement about her biological attributes and social status but an analysis of the all-important concept of woman as a being. If we can define woman, it may be possible to define man. Using man as point of departure when defining woman or life, will render interpretations invalid because woman's natural existence is more central than man's. Woman's status is demeaned and made out to be insignificant by male-dominant society, but this should not prevent us from forming a valid understanding of her reality.

Thus, it is clear that woman's physique is not deficient or inferior; on the contrary, the female body is more central than that of man. *This* is the root of man's extreme and meaningless jealousy.

The natural consequence of their differing physiques is that woman's emotional intelligence is much stronger than man's. Emotional intelligence is connected to life; it is the intelligence that governs empathy and sympathy. Even when woman's analytic intelligence develops, her emotional intelligence gives her the talent to live a balanced life, to be devoted to life and not to be destructive.

As can be seen even from this short discussion, man is a system. The male has *become* a state and turned this into the dominant culture. Class and sexual oppression develop together; masculinity has generated ruling gender, ruling class and ruling state. When man is analysed in this context, it is clear that masculinity must be killed.

Indeed, to kill the dominant man is the fundamental principle of socialism. This is what killing power means: to kill the one-sided domination, the inequality and intolerance. Moreover, it is to kill fascism, dictatorship and despotism. We should broaden this concept to include all these aspects.

Liberating life is impossible without a radical woman's revolution that would change man's mentality and life. If we are unable to make peace between man and life and life and woman, happiness is but a vain hope. Gender revolution is not just about woman. It is about the 5,000-year-old civilisation of class-based society which has left man worse off than woman. Thus, this gender revolution would simultaneously mean man's liberation.

I have often written about 'total divorce', i.e. the ability to divorce from the 5,000-year-old culture of male domination. The female and male gender identities that we know today are constructs that were formed much later than the biological female and male. Woman has been exploited for thousands of years according to this constructed identity; never acknowledged for her labour. Man has to overcome always seeing woman as wife, sister or lover – stereotypes forged by tradition and modernity.

Claiming that we first have to address the question of state *then* the question of family, is not sound. No serious social problem can be understood if addressed in isolation. A far more effective method is to look at everything within the totality, to render meaning to each question within its relationship to the other. This method also holds when we try to resolve problems. Analysing the social mentality without analysing the state, analysing the state without analysing the family, and analysing the woman without analysing the man would render insufficient results. We need to analyse these social phenomena as an integrated whole; if not, the solutions we arrive at will be inadequate.

The solutions to all social problems in the Middle East should have woman's position as their focus. The fundamental objective for the period ahead of us must be to realise the third major sexual rupture; this time against the male. Without gender equality, no demand for freedom and equality can be meaningful.

In fact, freedom and equality cannot be realised without the achievement of gender equality. The most permanent and comprehensive component of democratisation is woman's freedom. The societal system is most vulnerable because of the unresolved question of woman; woman who was first turned into property and who today is a commodity; completely, body and soul. The role the working class once played must now be taken over by the sisterhood of women. So, before we can analyse class, we must be able to analyse the sisterhood of women – this will enable us to form a much clearer understanding of the issues of class and nationality. Woman's true freedom is only possible if the enslaving emotions, needs and desires of husband, father, lover, brother, friend and son can all be removed. The deepest love constitutes the most dangerous bonds of ownership. We will not be able to discern the characteristics of a free woman if we cannot conduct a stringent critique of the thought, religious and art patterns concerning woman generated by the male-dominated world.

Woman's freedom cannot just be assumed once a society has obtained general freedom and equality. A separate and distinct organisation is essential, and woman's freedom should be of a magnitude equal to its definition as a phenomenon. Of course, a general democratisation movement may also uncover opportunities for women. But it will *not* bring democracy on its own. Women need to determine their own democratic aim, and institute the organisation and effort to realise it. To achieve this, a special definition of freedom is essential in order for woman to break free from the slavery ingrained in her.

JINEOLOJÎ AS THE SCIENCE OF WOMAN

The elimination of women from the ranks and the subjects of science requires us to look for a radical alternative.

We first need to know how to win within the ideological arena and to create a libertarian, natural mindset against the domineering, power-hungry mentality of the male. We should always keep in mind that the traditional female subjugation is not physical but social. It is due to ingrained slavery. Therefore, the most urgent need is to conquer the thoughts and emotions of subjugation within the ideological arena.

As the fight for woman's freedom heads towards the political arena, she should know that this is the most difficult aspect of the struggle. If success is not attained politically, no other achievement will be permanent. Being successful politically does not entail starting a movement for woman's statehood.

On the contrary, it entails struggling with statist and hierarchical structures; it entails creating political formations aiming to achieve a society that is democratic, gender equal, eco-friendly and where the state is not the pivotal element. Because hierarchy and statism are not easily compatible with woman's nature, a movement for woman's freedom should strive for anti-hierarchical and non-statist political formations. The collapse of slavery in the political arena is only possible if organisational reform in this area can be successfully attained. The political struggle requires a comprehensive, democratic organisation of woman and struggle. All components of civil society, human rights, local governance and democratic struggle should be organised and advanced. As with socialism, woman's freedom and equality can only be achieved through a comprehensive and successful democratic struggle. If democracy is not achieved, freedom and equality cannot be achieved either.

The issues related to economic and social equality can also be successfully resolved through an analysis of political power and through democratisation. A desiccated juridical equality means nothing in the absence of democratic politics; it will contribute nothing to the achievement of freedom. If the ownership and power relations which dominate and subjugate woman are not overthrown, then free relations between woman and man cannot be achieved either.

Although the feminist struggle has many important facets, it still has a long way to go to break down the limitations on democracy set by the West. Neither does it have a clear understanding of what the capitalist way of life entails. The situation is reminiscent of Lenin's understanding of socialist revolution.

Despite grand efforts and winning many positional battles, Leninism ultimately could not escape making the most precious left-wing contribution to capitalism.

A similar outcome may befall feminism. Deficiencies weakening its contention are: not having a strong organisational base; inability to develop its philosophy to the full; and difficulties relating to a militant woman's movement. It may not even be correct to call it 'the real socialism of women's front', but our analysis of this movement has to acknowledge that it has been the most serious measure to date to draw attention to the issue of woman's freedom. It does highlight that she is only the oppressed woman of the dominant man. However, woman's reality is much more comprehensive than just being a separate sex; it has economic, social and political dimensions. If we see colonialism not only in terms of nation and country but also in terms of groups of people, we can define woman as the oldest colonised group. Indeed, in both soul and body, no other social being has experienced such complete colonialism. It must be well understood that woman is kept in a colony with no easily identifiable borders.

In light of the above, I believe that the key to the resolution of our social problems will be a movement for woman's freedom, equality and democracy; a movement based on the science of woman, called *jineoloji* in Kurdish. The critique of recent women's movements is not sufficient for analysing and evaluating the history of civilisation and modernity that has made woman all but disappear. If, within the social sciences, there are almost no woman themes, questions and movements, then that is because of civilisation and modernity's hegemonic mentality and structures of material culture.

Moreover woman, as the prime component of moral and political society, has a critical role to play in forming an ethic and aesthetic of life that reflects freedom, equality and democratisation. Ethical and aesthetic science is an integral part of *jineoloji*. Because of her weighty responsibilities in life, she will no doubt be both the intellectual and implementation power behind developments and opportunities. Woman's link with life is more comprehensive than man's, and this has ensured the development of her emotional intelligence. Therefore aesthetics, in the sense of making life more beautiful, is an existential matter for woman. Ethically, woman is far more responsible than man. Thus, woman's behaviour with regard to morality and political society will be more realistic and responsible than man's. She is thus well suited to analyse, determine and decide on the good and bad aspects of education, the importance of life and peace, the malice and horror of war, and measures of appropriateness and justice. It would thus be appropriate to include economy in *jineoloji* as well.

DEMOCRATIC MODERNITY:
THE ERA OF WOMAN'S REVOLUTION

Woman's freedom will play a stabilising and equalising role in forming the new civilisation, and she will take her place under respectable, free and equal conditions. To achieve this, the necessary theoretical, programmatic, organisational and implementation work must be done. The reality of woman is a more concrete and analysable phenomenon than concepts such as 'proletariat' and 'oppressed nation'. The extent to which society can be thoroughly transformed is determined by the extent of the transformation attained by women. Similarly, the level of woman's freedom and equality determines the freedom and equality of all sections of society. Thus, the democratisation of woman is crucial for the permanent establishment of democracy and secularism. For a democratic nation, woman's freedom is of great importance too, as liberated woman constitutes liberated society. Liberated society in turn constitutes democratic nation. Moreover, the need to reverse the role of man is of revolutionary importance.

The dawn of the era of democratic civilisation represents not only the rebirth of peoples but, perhaps more distinctively, it represents the rise of woman. Woman, who was the creative goddess of Neolithic society, has encountered continuous losses throughout the history of classed society. Inverting this history will inevitably bring the most profound social results. Woman, reborn to freedom, will amount to general liberation, enlightenment and justice in all upper and lower institutions of society. This will convince all that peace, not war, is more valuable and is to be exalted. Woman's success is the success of society and the individual at all levels. The twenty-first century *must* be the era of awakening; the era of the liberated, emancipated woman. This is more important than class or national liberation. The era of democratic civilisation shall be the one when woman rises and succeeds fully.

It is realistic to see our century as the century when the will of the free woman will come to fruition. Therefore, permanent institutions for women need to be established and maintained for perhaps a century. There is a need for Woman's Freedom Parties. It is also vital that ideological, political and economic communes, based on woman's freedom, are formed.

Women in general, but more specifically Middle Eastern women, are the most energetic and active force in democratic society due to the characteristics described above. The ultimate victory of democratic society is only possible with women. Peoples and women have been devastated by classed society ever since the Neolithic age. They will now, as the pivotal agents of the democratic breakthrough, not only take revenge on history, but they will form the required anti-thesis by positioning themselves to the left of the rising democratic civilisation. Women are truly the most reliable social agents on the road to an equal and libertarian society. In the Middle East, it is up to the women and the youth to ensure the anti-thesis needed for the democratisation of society. Woman's awakening and being the leading societal force in this historical scene, has true antithetic value.

Due to the class characteristics of civilisations, their development has been based on male domination. This is what puts woman in this position of anti-thesis. In fact, in terms of overcoming the class divisions of society and male superiority, her position acquires the value of a new synthesis. Therefore, the leadership position of women's movements in the democratisation of Middle Eastern society has historical characteristics that make this both an anti-thesis (due to being in the Middle East) and a synthesis (globally). This area of work is the most crucial work that I have ever taken on. I believe it should have priority over the liberation of homelands and labour. If I am to be a freedom fighter, I cannot just ignore this: woman's revolution is a revolution within a revolution.

It is the fundamental mission of the new leadership to provide the power of intellect and will needed to attain the three aspects crucial for the realisation of a democratic modernity-system: a society that is democratic as well as economically and ecologically moral. To achieve this, we need to build a sufficient number of academic structures of appropriate quality. It is not enough merely to criticise the academic world of modernity – we have to develop an alternative. These alternative academic units should be constructed according to the priorities and the needs of all societal areas, such as economy and technology, ecology and agriculture, democratic politics, security and defence, culture, history, science and philosophy, religion and arts. Without a strong academic cadre, the elements of democratic modernity cannot be built. Academic cadres and elements of democratic modernity are equally important for attaining success. Interrelationship is a must to attain meaning and success.

The struggle for freedom (not only of women but of all ethnicities and different sections of the community) is as old as the enslavement and exploitation history of humanity. Yearning for freedom is intrinsic to human nature. Much has been learnt from these struggles, and from the battle we have been waging for the past 40 years. Democratic society has existed alongside different systems of mainstream civilisation. Democratic modernity, the alternative system to capitalist modernity, is possible through a radical change to our mentality and the corresponding, radical and appropriate changes in our material reality. These changes, we must build together.

Finally, I would like to point out that the struggle for women's freedom must be waged through the establishment of their own political parties, attaining a popular women's movement, building their own non-governmental organisations and structures of democratic politics. All these must be handled together, simultaneously. The better women are able to escape the grip of male domination and society, the better they will be able to act and live according to their independence initiative. The more women empower themselves, the more they regain their free personality and identity.

Therefore, giving support to women's ire, knowledge and freedom of movement is the greatest display of comradeship and a value of humanity. I have full confidence that women, irrespective of their different cultures and ethnicities, all those who have been excluded from the system, will succeed. The twenty-first century shall be the century of women's liberation.

I hope to make my own contributions – not only by writing on these issues, but by helping to implement the changes.

4

Democratic Nation

INTRODUCTION

Until now, the PKK's struggle has essentially been aimed at making the Kurdish question visible. The denial of Kurdish reality during the time of its formation naturally brought the question of existence on to the agenda. Thus, the PKK at first tried to prove the existence of the question, by means of ideological arguments. The continuation of this denial by the left, through more refined methods, put organising on the basis of separate identities and action on the agenda.

The Turkish nation-state – which insisted on traditional denial and annihilation policies – refused to consider the possibility of a political solution during this period. On the contrary, it chose to counter the PKK's initiatives with a campaign of fascist terror that led up to the 12 September coup. The PKK's declaration of a revolutionary people's war emerged as the only viable option. Under these conditions, the PKK was either going to wither away, like the other democratic left groups in Turkey, or decide on resistance. The decisive factor in the transformation of the Kurdish question from being one of ideological identity into a question of war is the state's insistence on maintaining previously covert policies of denial and annihilation through the open terror of 12 September. It would be more realistic to analyse the offensive of 15 August 1984 within this framework. Such a move is much closer to the objective of proving the existence of the Kurdish people and protecting their existence than of being a liberation movement. It should be pointed out that, in this regard, it has attained a significant success.

The PKK, while proving Kurdish existence beyond any doubt, got stuck in nation-statism. The ensuing period of self-criticism revealed the anti-socialist and anti-democratic essence of nation-statism. The speedy dissolution of real socialism in the 1990s contributed to a deeper understanding of the underlying factors behind the crisis. The dissolution of real socialism was caused by power and real socialist nation-state problematics. To be more precise, the crisis of socialism was the result of an inadequate understanding of the problem of power and the state. When the contradictions of state and power, set out so starkly by the Kurdish question, coalesced with the wider global crisis of real socialism, a comprehensive analysis of the issue of the state and power became inevitable.

To this end, in a significant part of my defence, I tried to analyse the state and power throughout civilisational history. I concentrated on presenting the transformation of the phenomena of state and power in the context of capitalist modernity – the present-day hegemonic civilisation. I specifically argued that the transformation of power into the nation-state was the basis of capitalism. This was an important thesis. I tried to demonstrate that in the absence of power being organised through the nation-state model, capitalism could not have become the new hegemonic system. The nation-state was the fundamental tool that made capitalist hegemony possible. Therefore, I tried to prove that socialism, as anti-capitalism, presenting itself as what I call 'historical society', could not establish itself as based on the same state model, in other words, as a real socialist nation-state. I tried to show that the idea that socialism, as proposed by Marx and Engels, could only be constructed through central nation-states was indeed a fundamental defect of scientific socialism. I went on to present the thesis that socialism could not be constructed through the state, especially the nation-state, and that an insistence on this could only result in the most degenerate versions of capitalism as experienced in many instances, but especially in the actually existing socialism of Russia and China. As a necessary precursor to this thesis, I analysed the system of central civilisation throughout history, the concept of power, and the structure of capitalist modernity's state and power which is the prevalent structure unique to our era. My main conclusion was that socialists could not have a nation-state principle. Rather, the solution to the national question should be based on the principle of the democratic nation. The practical expression of this, as I will try to show, is the KCK (Union of Democratic Communities in Kurdistan) experience.

Kurdistan, in a way, has already become the focus of revolution and counter-revolution in the twenty-first century. It is the weakest link of capitalist modernity. The national and social problems of the people of Kurdistan have become so aggravated that they cannot be concealed by means of liberal prescriptions or the demagogy of individual or cultural rights. When it comes to the Kurdish question, nation-statism – which led to different practices, including cultural genocide – is no longer a problem-solver; rather, it has long been the source of the problem, both for the oppressor and the oppressed. Nation-statism is in dissolution and it has even become a problem for capitalist modernity. More flexible democratic national developments will spearhead the advances of our era. Democratic modernity signifies the theoretical expression and the practical steps of these advances. The KCK, as the concrete expression of democratic national transformations in Kurdistan, sheds light on the path of democratic modernity solution in the Middle East.

CAPITALIST MODERNITY AND THE NATION

The nation, as a concept, comes after entities such as clan and tribe with kinship in the form of people and nationality, and is a social form generally characterised by linguistic or cultural similarities. National communities are more inclusionary and have larger capacities than clans and people's communities; for this reason, they are human communities with looser ties to one another. National society is more a phenomenon of our time. If a general definition can be offered, it is a community of those who share a common mindset. In other words, it is a phenomenon that exists mentally, which therefore means it is an abstract and imagined phenomenon. We can also call this a culturally defined nation. Sociologically speaking, this would be the correct definition. Despite differing class, gender, colour, ethnicity and even national background, in the most general sense the formation of a shared mindset and culture is enough to be classified as a nation.

In order to refine this general definition of nation, generated concepts such as state nation, legal nation, economic nation and military nation are different categories of nationalism that are used to underpin the understanding of this general definition of nation. It could also be called 'power nation'. It is a fundamental aspiration of capitalist modernity to become a strong nation, in as much as a strong nation produces capital privilege, a comprehensive market, colonial opportunities and imperialism. It is, therefore, important not to accept these robust versions as the only possible models of a nation. In fact, it is important to see these power nations as nations in the service of capital. These are the qualities that make the nation-state the source of the problems I am interested in here.

The main problem in the age of modernity derives from the coupling of power and state with the nation. When we compare the problems of this age with the problems of dictatorships and dynastic states, we can see that the problems of the age of modernity derive from the 'state nation'; this is the biggest difference between the ages. The nation-state is one of the most convoluted subjects within the social sciences, yet it is presented as the tool to solve all the problems that face modernity, like a magic wand. In essence, it only multiplies social problems, because it spreads its power apparatus into the capillaries of societies. Power itself creates problems – it generates social problems because of the potential character of capital that has been organised by force, which results in suppression and exploitation. The homogeneous nation society to which the nation-state aspires can only construct artificially (supposedly legal) equal citizens, charged with violence as a result of being amputated by power. These citizens may be equal in the eyes of the law, but they experience maximum inequality in every aspect of life as individuals and as a collective entity.

When analysing the theory of nation, another aspect that needs to be critically evaluated is the sacralisation and deification of the nation. Capitalist modernity has replaced traditional religion and God and constructed the deified nation-state. If we interpret nationalism as the religion of the nation-state, then we can perceive the nation-state itself to be the god of this religion. The state has been constructed in the age of modernity in order to incorporate the essence of medieval and even antiquarian conceptualisations of divinity. The phenomenon called the 'secular state' is the construction of medieval and antiquarian divinities as state either in whole or in essence. There should be no confusion here. Once you scrape off the secular or modern nation-state veneer, you encounter the divine state of antiquity and the medieval age. There is a strong correlation between state and divinity. In the same manner, there is a very strong relationship between the rising monarch of antiquity and the medieval age and the concept of God. After the medieval age, when the monarch lost his significance, both as an individual and in terms of the monarchy, and began to institutionalise and transmute into the national state, the god-monarch was replaced by the nation-state god. Therefore, capitalist modernity's ideological hegemony, which makes the attainment of maximum profit possible, is what underlies the sacralisation of concepts such as the homeland, nation and market, together with a similar sacralisation of nation-state institutions. The law of maximum profit becomes more legitimate as the concepts related to the nation are religionised by the ideological hegemony and thus validated.

In our age, the use of nation-state symbols and fundamental slogans such as 'one flag', 'one language', 'one homeland', 'one state' and 'unitary state', and the expression of national chauvinism, are ramped up and turned into rituals at every opportunity, especially at sporting events or during art activities, should be interpreted as the means of worshipping the religion of nationalism. In fact, the practice of worship in previous ages served the same purpose.

The main objective here is to validate the interests of monopolies of power and exploitation through concealing or legitimising them. We will be better able to understand the truth of societal reality once we interpret all the practices and approaches that serve to hide or exaggerate those things related to the nation-state under this fundamental paradigm.

The organisation of capitalist modernity as nation-state plays a much more suppressive and exploitative role then its organisation as an economic monopoly. The inability of Marxism, and sociology in general, to see the nation-state's relationship with suppression and exploitation, or its presentation of the nation-state as an ordinary institution of the superstructure, is a fundamental flaw and distortion. When an analysis of class and material capital is made independent of the nation-state, what's being produced is a stale and abstract generalisation that cannot generate a useful social result. Such abstractions, and their consequences, underlie the failure of real socialism.

That the solution to all national and social problems is linked to the nation-state represents the most tyrannical aspect of modernity. To expect a solution from the tool which is itself the source of the problem can only lead to further problems and societal chaos. Capitalism itself is the most crisis-ridden stage of civilisation. The nation-state, as the tool deployed in this crisis-ridden stage, is the most developed organisation of violence in social history. It is society besieged by the violence of power; it is the tool deployed forcefully to hold society and the environment together after they have been disintegrated through industrialism and capitalism's law of maximum profit. The reason it is excessively charged with violence is due to the capitalist system's tendency for maximum profit and uninterrupted accumulation. Without an organisation of violence like the nation-state, the laws of capitalist accumulation could not operate and industrialism could not be maintained. Society and the environment are on the brink of total disintegration in this present era of global financial capitalism. The crises, which were initially cyclical, have now attained a structural and permanent character. Under these circumstances, the nation-state itself has turned into an obstacle that locks the system down completely. Even capitalism, which is a crisis-ridden system itself, has made getting rid of the obstacle of the nation-state a priority. The sovereignty of the nation-state is not only the cause of societal problems, but is the main obstacle to finding solutions.

The theory of democratic modernity, on the other hand, is not only critical of capitalism's political economy, but of its whole system. Democratic modernity criticises capitalism's relationship with civilisational history as a hegemonic system; the changes it has caused in city, class and state; and the elements upon which it constructs its modernity in order to uncover its reality. Capitalist modernity continuously legitimises itself through the ideological hegemony it establishes over science, philosophy and the arts. By instrumentalising these fundamental fields of thought and draining them of their content, it deepens its destruction of society.

DEMOCRATIC MODERNITY

The alternative modernity for the democratic nation is democratic modernity. An economy free of monopolism, an ecology that signifies harmony with the environment, and a technology that is friendly to nature and humanity are the institutional bases of democratic modernity and thus the democratic nation. I have neither discovered nor invented democratic modernity. Democratic modernity, since the formation of official civilisation, has always existed as its counterpart in a dichotomy. It has existed wherever and whenever an official civilisation has existed. What I am trying to do, albeit as a rough outline, is to give this other form of modernity – which exists at each location and time alongside official civilisation – the recognition it deserves, and offer explanations in terms of its main dimensions. I am also trying to understand its fundamental forms of mindset, its structures and its existing society, and to define them. There is nothing baffling about the idea that, according to dialectics, there exists a counterpart to civilisation, although alleged to be singular, at all places and periods that it has existed. To the contrary, the baffling thing is why this most natural equivalent of dialectical method has not been systematically articulated.

Democratic modernity, though it has changed form according to different eras, has always existed and is a reality that has always had its own counter-history throughout civilisational history. It signifies the system of universal history that is outside of the forces of tyranny and exploitation. Kurdish reality represents a culture that has received the severest blows from civilisational forces, and is a culture that has been attacked by forces intent on exterminating it. Therefore, it can only realise its existence through a civilisation which is outside traditional classed civilisation – as a democratic socialist civilisation. If a meaningful Kurdish history is to be written, it can only be done so within this framework. The present-day expression of this is democratic modernity.

Democratic modernity responds to the universalist, linear, pro-gressivist and determinist methodology (the methodological approach that is closed to probabilities and alternatives) deployed by the modern nation-state to achieve the homogenisation and her-dification of society with methods that are pluralistic, probabilistic, open to alternatives and that can make democratic society visible. It develops its alternative through its properties of being open to different political formations, multicultural, closed to monopolism, ecological and feminist, creating an economic structure that is grounded in satisfying society's fundamental needs and is at the disposal of the community. As opposed to capitalist modernity's nation-state, democratic confederalism is democratic modernity's political alternative.

Democratic confederalism is the basic political format of democratic modernity; it plays a vital role in reconstruction work and is the most appropriate tool for helping democratic politics generate a solution. Democratic confederalism presents the option of a democratic nation as the fundamental tool to resolve the ethnic, religious, urban, local, regional and national problems caused by the monolithic, homogeneous, monochrome, fascist social model implemented by modernity's nation-state. Within the democratic nation every ethnicity, religious understanding and city, local, regional and national entity has the right to participate with its own identity and democratic federate structure.

DEMOCRATIC SOLUTION

There have always been attempts to solve the national problems caused by capitalist modernity by nation-statist and nationalist mindsets and paradigms. The nation-state itself has been presented as the main factor in providing a solution. In order to gain a true understanding of the nation-state one must understand its place in the hegemonic system and its links to capitalism and industrialism. The inadequate analysis of the question of state by socialist ideology only obscures the problem further. However, in 'the right of nations to self-determination', the vision of a state for every nation was fundamental in aggravating the issue even more.

The essence of my defence is to research the Kurdish reality and Kurdish people's existence in relation to civilisation and modernity. The aim is to explain that capitalism was primarily responsible for the rise of the Kurdish question and to separate the democratic essence of the solution from nation-statism for the first time. This approach constitutes the essence of the transformation within the PKK. This defence explains the difference between forms of statist and democratic solutions that have not been clarified since the PKK's group phase. This is where it differs from real socialism and the classic Marxist-Leninist doctrine behind it. It takes the right of nations to self-determination from its enclosure as a bourgeois right, and includes it within the scope of societal democracy. In other words, the Kurdish question could be solved without being contaminated by statism, without gravitating towards a nation-statist pursuit and, without being forced into solutions under these categories, it could be resolved within democratic governance models of society. This is the essence of the transformation of the PKK.

The democratic solution model is not just an option, it is the primary method for achieving a solution. The democratic solution signifies the pursuit of the democratisation of society outside of the nation-state. As a concept, it sees the nation-state, along with capitalism, as the source of ever-increasing problems and not the solution in relation to social problems. One should not think of the democratic solution model as a unitary nation-state that has been transformed into a federal or confederal form. The federal or confederal state of the nation-state is not the *democratic solution*. These are solutions that rely on different forms of the state, and yet only aggravate the problem. Perhaps the transformation of a rigidly centralised nation-state into federal or confederal forms within the capitalist system's mindset may ameliorate problems and offer partial solutions, but it cannot lead to comprehensive solutions. Federal and confederal forms can be deployed as possible solutions between the nation-statist forces and the forces for a democratic solution. However, to expect a deep-rooted solution as a result will only lead yet again to self-deception. Indeed, we know that states described as national liberationist states or real socialist states are just nation-states with a leftist mask.

It is important to note that the democratic solution method is not completely independent of the nation-state. Democracy and the nation-state can play a role under the same political roof as two authorities. A democratic constitution can determine the domain for each of them. A positive transformation of the nation-state is closely linked to the development of democratisation and democratic autonomous governance, and the construction of the democratic nation, local democracy and democratic culture in all social spheres.

The KCK should be evaluated as a radical transformation in the solution to the national question as it represents the non-statist democratic interpretation of the right of nations to self-determination for the Kurdish question. KCK is the concrete expression of the democratic solution to the Kurdish question and differs from traditional approaches. The solution is not regarded as taking a share from the state. It is not in the pursuit of state, even in terms of autonomy for the Kurds. Not only does it not aim for a federal or confederal state, it does not see them as the solution. Its main demand from the state is for it to recognise the Kurdish people's right to self-governance and to remove the obstacles in the way of the Kurdish people becoming a democratic nation. The democratic solution cannot be developed by governments or states. Societal forces are themselves solely responsible for developing the solution. Societal forces seek to find a compromise with the government or the state through a democratic constitution. The sharing of governance between democratic societal forces and the state or government forces is determined through constitutions.

Essentially, the democratic solution is the state of being a democratic nation and of society constructing itself as a democratic national entity. It is neither becoming a nation nor ceasing to be a nation through the state; it is the ability to use the right of a society to construct itself as a democratic nation. At this stage, a new definition of the nation must be created. First, it is worth noting that the term nation does not have a single definition. I touched on this above. The democratic nation, on the other hand, is the common society formed by the free will of free individuals and communities. The unifying factor in the democratic nation is the free will of the people and those groups who decide to belong to that nation. The understanding that binds the nation to a common language, culture, market or history is descriptive of nation-states and cannot be generalised, that is, it cannot be reduced to a single understanding of the nation. This understanding of nation, which was also acknowledged by real socialism, is the opposite of the democratic nation. This definition, as developed by Stalin for Soviet Russia, is one of the main reasons for the dissolution of the Soviet Union. If this definition of nation, absolutised by capitalist modernity, is not abandoned, then the solution to all national problems will continue to meet an impasse. The fact that national problems have persisted for the past three centuries is closely linked to this inadequate and absolute definition.

THE DEMOCRATIC NATION MODEL

For societies, the nation-state model is nothing but a pitfall and network of suppression and exploitation. The democratic nation concept reverses this definition. The definition of a democratic nation that is not bound by rigid political boundaries and a single language, culture, religion and interpretation of history, signifies plurality and communities as well as free and equal citizens existing together and in solidarity. The democratic nation allows the people to become a nation themselves, without relying on power and state – becoming a nation through much-needed politicisation. It aims to prove that in the absence of becoming a state or acquiring power, and without politicisation, a nation can be created with autonomous institutions in the social, diplomatic and cultural spheres as well as in economy, law and self-defence, and thus build itself as a democratic nation.

Democratic society can only be realised through such a nation model. The nation-state society is closed to democracy by its very nature. The nation-state represents neither a universal nor a local reality; on the contrary, it disavows universality and locality. The citizenship of a uniformised society represents the death of the human. On the other hand, the democratic nation makes the recon-struction of universality and locality possible. It enables societal reality to express itself. All other definitions of nation lie between these two main models.

Although there is a wide range of definitions for nation-building models, an all-encompassing definition is also possible; and this is the definition of nation in relation to its mindset, consciousness and belief. In this case, the nation is a community of people who share a common mindset. In such a definition of nation, language, religion, culture, market, history and political borders play not a decisive but a bodily role. Defining nation essentially as a certain mindset gives it a dynamic character. Whereas in nation-states nationalism leaves its mark on the common mindset, in a democratic nation it is the consciousness of freedom and solidarity. However, defining nations only through their mindset would be incomplete. Just as mindsets cannot exist without bodies, nations too cannot function without a body. The body of nations with a nationalist mindset is the state institution. This is why such nations are called nation-states. When legal and economic institutions outweigh the rest, these nations can be differentiated by categorising them as law or market nations.

Nations with a mindset based on freedom and solidarity exemplify democratic autonomy. Democratic autonomy essentially denotes the self-governance of communities and individuals who share a similar mindset through their own will. This could also be called democratic governance or authority. It is a definition open to universality. A nation model that can be derived from the concept of a 'culture nation', but which kerbs and excludes exploitation and suppression, is a democratic nation model. A democratic nation is the nation closest to freedom and equality. And in accordance with this definition, this is the ideal understanding of nation for communities who strive for freedom and equality.

Capitalist modernity, and the science of sociology that it has inspired, has not dealt with the concept of the democratic nation due to its structure and ideological hegemony. The democratic nation is not content with a common mindset and culture – it is a nation that unifies and governs all its members in democratic autonomous institutions. This is its defining quality. The democratic autonomous way of governance is the foremost condition of becoming a democratic nation. In this regard, it is the alternative to the nation-state. Democratic governance as opposed to state governance is a significant opportunity for freedom and equality. Liberal sociology equates the nation either with an already established state, or with a movement that aims to establish a state. The fact that even real socialism had such ambitions shows the strength of liberal ideology.

A common homeland and market are generally presented as pre-conditions for national societies; these are material components and cannot be considered to be determinant characteristics of the nation. The democratic nation's understanding of homeland and market are different. The democratic nation values the homeland because it is hugely important for the nation's mindset and culture; a mindset and culture that does not keep the homeland in mind can not be imagined. However, it should not be forgotten that the reason why capitalist modernity fetishises and prioritises the country-homeland concept over society is profit-motivated. It is also important not to exaggerate the homeland. 'Everything for the country' derives from a fascistic understanding of the nation. It is more meaningful to devote everything to a free society and a democratic nation, but this should not be fetishised. What really matters is to render life valuable. The homeland isn't an ideal, it is merely a tool for the life of the individual and the nation. While the state's nation pursues homogenised society, the democratic nation mainly consists of different collectivities. It sees diversity as richness. Life itself is only possible through diversity. The nation-state forces citizens to be uniform; in this regard, too, it is contrary to life. The ultimate goal is to create a robotic human. In this sense, it actually runs towards nothingness. The citizen or member of the democratic nation is different, and this difference is due to the diverse communities it embodies. Tribal entities are a source of strength for the democratic nation.

Although language is as important as culture in creating a nation, it is not a precondition. Different languages are no obstacle to a sense of belonging to the same nation. Just as it is unnecessary for every nation to have a state, it is also unnecessary for every nation to have a single language or dialect. Although a national language is needed, it is not an indispensable condition. It is possible to count different languages and dialects as a source of richness for a democratic nation. However, the nation-state bases itself on a strict imposition of a single language. It does not easily give multilingualism, especially official multilingualism, a chance to be practised. In this regard, it tries to benefit from the privileges of being the dominant nation.

When democratic nations are unable to develop and nation-statism is unable to resolve problems, it is possible to talk of a law nation as a concept and to find a compromise. What is meant by 'constitutional citizenship' is actually a solution based on the law nation. A constitutionally guaranteed legal citizenship does not discriminate between race, ethnicity and nationality. These characteristics do not accord rights. In this regard, 'law nation' is a developing category. European nations in particular are transitioning from nationality nations to law nations. In democratic nations, autonomous governance is fundamental; in a law nation, rights are fundamental; whereas in the nation-state, it is the rule of power that is decisive. The most dangerous nation type is the 'army nation' mindset and its institutionalisation. Although it may seem as if it represents a strong nation, in essence it is the most difficult nation to live in, containing a mindset that always imposes duties and leads to fascism. The economic nation is a category very similar to the nation-state. This understanding of a nation, seen in countries such as the USA, Japan and even Germany, where the economy is given a leading role, was more prevalent in Europe's past. Although a socialist nation was attempted, it can't be said that it was very successful. This is partially what we are witnessing in Cuba. However, this example of a nation is also the real socialist form of the nation-state; in place of a nation-state with mostly private capitalism, it is a nation-state form that contains mostly state capitalism.

The democratic nation is the model of a nation that is the least exposed to such illnesses of being a state nation. It does not sacralise its government. Governance is a simple phenomenon that is at the service of daily life. Anyone who meets the requirements can become a public servant and govern. Leadership is valuable, but not sacred. Its understanding of national identity is open-ended, not fixed like being a believer or a member of a religion. Belonging to a nation is neither a privilege nor a flaw. One can belong to more than one nation. To be more precise, one can experience intertwined and different nationalities. If a law nation and a democratic nation reach a compromise, they can comfortably coexist. Homeland, flag and language are all valuable but not sacred. To experience the admixture of common homeland, languages and flags through amity and sharing and not confrontation is not only possible, but necessary for historical society life. With all these characteristics, the democratic nation is once again taking its place in history as a robust alternative to capitalist modernity's maddening instrument of war: nation-statism.

The democratic nation model, as a constructive solution model, redemocratises those societal relations that have been shattered by nation-statism; it renders different identities tolerant, peaceful and reconciliatory. The evolution of nation-states into democratic nations will bring about enormous gains. The democratic nation model ameliorates violence-loaded social perceptions through a caring social consciousness and renders them humane (a human being who is intelligent, sensitive and empathetic). It may not completely eliminate social antipathies but it can minimise the violence of exploitation, and help to realise the possibility of a more equal and free society. It not only fosters internal peace and tolerance, it also transcends suppressive and exploitative approaches to other nations and transforms common interests into synergies through which it realises its mission. Once national and international institutions are reconstructed according to the fundamental mindset and institutions of the democratic nation, it will be understood that this new modernity, democratic modernity, has the attributes of a renaissance not only theoretically but also in its implementation. The alternative to capitalist modernity is democratic modernity, with the democratic nation at its core, and the economic, ecological and peaceful society it has woven within and outside of the democratic nation.

Kurds Becoming a Nation

It is possible to think of the process through which the Kurds became a nation in the context of two fundamental concepts.

The first is the mental, or the dimension of the Kurdish mindset. They will not neglect their own language, culture, history, economy or population growth. But at the same time they will unite their state of consciousness with a feeling of joint solidarity in relation to these fundamental areas. We are thus talking about the dimensions of existence of those that share such a mindset. The main characteristic of this dimension is that people share the mindset of an ideal, free and equal world based on diversity. We can call this world the communal world, or a utopia of free individuals. The important thing is to *continuously* maintain a mindset of freedom and equality that does not reject differences within the public sphere or the moral and political life of society.

Because the mental dimension concerns the world of thought and imagination as well as the solidarity of individuals and communities wanting to become a nation, it requires a limited rearrangement. To this end, developing education in science, philosophy and art (including religion), and opening schools with this objective, are the foremost practical steps; intellectual and emotional education in relation to becoming a nation is the task of these schools. It is essential to understand social culture in relation to our current epoch, just as much as in relation to the historical-societal entity, and to share true, good and beautiful aspects in common thoughts and emotions. In a nutshell, the KCK's main intellectual task is to envisage the Kurds as a nation within their *true, good* and *beautiful* world of thought and emotions jointly shared in relation to their own existence. In other words, its task is to encourage the Kurdish people to become a nation by means of a scientific, philosophical and artistic revolution, and to create the fundamental conditions (intellectual and emotional) for becoming such a nation, freely sharing the scientific, philosophical (ideological) and artistic truth of Kurdish reality. The way to go about realising this is through self-thought and self-education, sharing the good and living well. The main thing demanded of the sovereign nation-states in terms of the intellectual dimension, is for them to adhere fully to freedom of expression and thought. If nation-states want to coexist with the Kurds under common norms, then they must respect the Kurdish people's desire to create their own intellectual and emotional world and to turn themselves into a national society on the basis of their own differences: the freedom of expression and thought required for this must be constitutionally guaranteed.

The second dimension is the reorganisation of social existence in accordance with its mental world. How is society to be reorganised in accordance with the intellectual world of a nation that is shared commonly? Democratic autonomy lies at the heart of the reorganisation of this physical existence. It is possible to define democratic autonomy in both a broad and narrow sense. In the broadest sense, democratic autonomy is the expression of the democratic nation. The democratic nation has dimensions divided across a wider range. It can be defined in terms of its cultural, economic, social, legal, diplomatic and other dimensions. In the narrow sense, democratic autonomy represents the political dimension; in other words, it means democratic authority or governance. The democratic autonomy dimension of becoming a democratic nation is much more problematic in terms of relations with sovereign nation-states. Sovereign nation-states generally reject democratic autonomy. They do not wish to recognise it as a right unless they are obliged to do so. With regard to the Kurds, the acceptance of democratic autonomy lies at the heart of a reconciliation with nation-states. Democratic autonomy is the minimum requirement to live under the common political roof of a nation-state with a dominant ethnicity. Anything less would lead to an increase in conflict and a worsening of the situation – not a solution. Especially lately, there has been an effort to implement the liberal 'individual and cultural rights' project – originally developed by English capitalism in order to rule their working class and colonies – in the Republic of Turkey via Adalet ve Kalkınma Partisi (the Justice and Development Party). This project, which is alien to Middle Eastern culture, will only serve to expand the conflict. Democratic autonomy is the most suitable solution for the nation-state. Anything less would only fuel further conflict and war.

The Democratic Autonomy Solution and its Implementation

The democratic autonomy solution can be implemented in two ways. The first is predicated on finding a compromise with nation-states. It finds its concrete expression in a democratic constitutional solution. It respects the historical-societal heritage of peoples and cultures. It regards the freedom of expression and organisation of these heritages as irrevocable and fundamental constitutional rights. Democratic autonomy is the fundamental principle of these rights. The foremost conditions of this arrangement are that the sovereign nation-state renounces all denial and annihilation policies, and the oppressed nation abandons the idea of forming its own nation-state. It is difficult for a democratic autonomy project to be implemented without both nations renouncing statist tendencies in this regard. EU countries took more than 300 years of nation-state experience before they could accept democratic autonomy as the best solution for solving nation-states' regional, national and minority-related problems.

In the solution to the Kurdish question, too, the path that is meaningful and consistent is the one that does not rely on separatism and violence and that accepts democratic autonomy. All other paths will either lead to a delay in addressing problems, and therefore to a deepening of the impasse, or to violent conflict and separation. The history of national problems is littered with such examples. The relative peace, wealth and prosperity of the EU countries – the home of national conflicts – during the past 60 years was achieved due to their acceptance of democratic autonomy and their ability to find flexible and creative solutions to regional, national and minority problems. The opposite has been true of the Republic of Turkey. The nation-statism that it was hoped would be completed through the denial and annihilation of the Kurds has drawn Turkey to the brink of disintegration, with continuous crises, regular military coups and a special warfare regime that is conducted together with Gladio.[1] Only when the Turkish nation-state abandons these policies, and accepts the democratic autonomy of all cultures (including Turkish and Turkmens), and specifically the Kurdish cultural entity's

---

1 Operation Gladio (Italian, *Operazione Gladio*) is the codename for a clandestine North Atlantic Treaty Organisation (NATO) 'stay-behind' operation in Italy during the Cold War. Turkey was one of the first countries to participate.

democratic autonomy, will it achieve lasting peace and prosperity as a normal, lawful, secular and democratic republic.

The second path for a democratic autonomy solution – one that does not depend on finding a compromise with nation-states – is to implement its own project unilaterally. In a broad sense, this path recognises the Kurdish people's right to become a democratic nation through the implementation of democratic autonomy. It goes without saying that in this case conflicts will intensify with those sovereign nation-states who do not accept this unilateral implementation of becoming a democratic nation. If this happens, the Kurds will have no other choice but to adopt a full-scale mobilisation and war position in order to protect their existence and to live freely against the individual or joint attacks of nation-states (Iran, Syria and Turkey). They will not hold back from becoming a democratic nation with all its dimensions and to develop and realise their aspirations through their own efforts until they either reach a compromise or achieve independence amid the warfare.

The KCK and the Dimensions of Becoming a Democratic Nation

In light of these general definitions of the nation, the KCK rejects state nationist approaches and bases itself on the democratic nationist model, acknowledging the Kurdish people's right to become a nation and to achieve their transformation into a national society through democratic autonomy.

If we liken societies, especially the democratic nations of our era, to a living organism, then we can say that all its parts and dimensions are interconnected and coexist as in the integral whole of a live organism. Therefore, although each and every dimension is discussed in their own right, they must always be considered as parts of a whole.

THE FREE INDIVIDUAL-CITIZEN AND DEMOCRATIC COMMUNAL LIFE

The individual-citizen of a democratic nation has to be communal as well as free. The allegedly free individual of capitalist individualism, who has been provoked into being at odds with society, essentially lives a life of abject slavery. However, liberal ideology creates an image where the individual apparently possesses limitless freedom. In reality the individual, enslaved by waged labour, represents the most developed form of slavery. This type of individual is produced through the relentless education of, and life in, nation-statism. Because his or her life is bound to the sovereignty of money, the wage system, in effect like a dog's leash, ensures that the individual can be manipulated as desired: he or she has no other means of surviving. If they seek to escape – that is, if they opt for unemployment – it is in effect a death sentence. Moreover, capitalist individualism has been shaped on the basis of society's denial. The individual thinks that they can only realise themself insofar as they reject the culture and traditions of historical society. This is the biggest distortion of liberal ideology. Its principal slogan is 'there is no society, there is only the individual'.

As opposed to this, the democratic nation's individual sees his or her freedom in the communality of society, in the form of the more functional life of small communities. A free and democratic commune or community is the main school in which the individual in a democratic nation takes shape. Without a commune or communal life, the individual cannot be fully realised. Communes are diverse and valid in every sphere of societal life. In accordance with their diversity, individuals can exist in more than one commune or community. The important thing is for the individual to know how to live in a communal community in accordance with his or her talents, labour and diversity. The individual considers the responsibility towards the commune or the social units to which they are attached to be their guiding moral principle. Morality means respect and commitment to the community and to communal life. The commune or community in turn protects the individual and enhances his or her life. After all, the fundamental principle behind the founding of human society is this very principle of moral responsibility. The democratic character of the commune or communities is what realises the collective freedom – in other words, the political commune or community. A commune or community that is not democratic cannot be political.

A commune or community that is not political therefore cannot be free. There is a close correlation between the political and democratic character of the commune and its freedom.

The definition of the democratic nation's individual-citizen becomes slightly broader when he or she lives under the same political roof as a nation-state. In this case, within the framework of 'constitutional citizenship', she is as much an individual-citizen of the nation-state as she is of the democratic nation. The point here is the recognition of the status of the democratic nation, whereby democratic autonomy is acknowledged to have legal status in the national constitution. Democratic national status is twofold. First, it denotes the status, law and constitution of democratic autonomy. Second, autonomy is incorporated as a subsection of the national constitutional status.

Although the unilateral construction of a democratic nation based on the free individual-citizen and the communal unity of the KCK is a priority, it is also possible for the KCK to arrive at an agreement with those sovereign nation-states who acknowledge the status of democratic autonomy within the national democratic constitution. The KCK recognises both the life of the free individual-citizen and community and the extent to which this life is bound by a legal and constitutional status.

Capitalist individualism requires absolute servitude to the nation-state god, whereas democratic nation citizenship fosters the development of the free individual in the truest sense. The democratic nation citizenship of the Kurds can be realised under the KCK status. Therefore, it may be more appropriate to define membership of the KCK as being democratic nation citizenship. It is an irrevocable right and duty for the Kurdish people to be citizens of their own democratic nation. To be unable to be a citizen of one's own nation is a huge alienation and is indefensible.

POLITICAL LIFE AND DEMOCRATIC AUTONOMY

It is possible to define the school of social sciences that studies the ontology and development of societal nature on the basis of moral and political society as the 'democratic civilisation system school'. Determining moral and political society to be our fundamental unit is also important, as this comprises the dimensions of historicity and integrality. Moral and political society is the most historical and holistic narrative of society. Morality and politics can be seen as history itself. A society with a moral and political dimension is a society that is in harmony with its existence and development. Society can exist without exploitation, classes, cities, power, nation and the state, but a society devoid of morals and politics is unthinkable.

A moral and political society is a democratic society. Democracy can only attain meaning on the basis of the existence of an open and free society; that is, a moral and political society. Democratic society, where individuals and groups become subjects, corresponds with a form of governance that most effectively develops moral and political society. More precisely, the functionality of political society is what we already call democracy. Politics and democracy, in the true sense, are identical concepts. If freedom is the arena in which politics expresses itself, then democracy is the modus operandi of politics within that arena. The trio of freedom, politics and democracy cannot be devoid of a moral base. We can also define morals as the institutionalised or traditional form of freedom, politics and democracy.

Moral and political societies are in dialectical contradiction with the state, which is the official expression of all forms of capital, ownership and power. The state constantly desires to replace morals with law, and politics with bureaucratic administration. On the twin poles of this historical contradiction, the official state civilisation and the unofficial democratic civilisation coexist. Two separate typologies of meaning emerge. The contradictions can either intensify and lead to war, or reconcile and lead to peace.

Today, the problematic nature of nation-states is propelling political societies and their governing forces towards becoming democratic nations, either through reform or revolution. While nation-states were the dominant tendency during the rise of capitalism, under the current conditions of its downfall the dominant tendency is to evolve towards becoming democratic nations. In this regard, it is important not to equate political force with state power. Politics cannot be equated with power and its institutionalised form, the state. Freedom is in the nature of politics. Politicised societies and nations are societies and nations that are becoming free.

Politics not only liberates, it also regulates. Politics is a unique regulatory force; is a kind of art. It represents the opposite of the suppressive regulations of states and rulers. The stronger the politics in a society or nation, the weaker the state and ruling powers. The opposite is also true: the stronger the state or ruling power is in a society or nation, the weaker the politics – and hence freedom – in that society.

Just as a society or nation that gains state and ruling power does not become free even if there were any democratic features, it also faces the prospect of losing whatever freedoms it previously had. This is why the more we remove state and power from society, the more we open it up to freedom. And the fundamental condition that is necessary for liberating that society and nation is for it to maintain itself in a permanent political position.

It will be seen that the democratic civilisation system has always existed and sustained itself as the other face of official civilisation's history, in essence as the moral and political unity of societal nature. Despite suppression and exploitation by the official world system, the other face of society could not be eliminated. In any case, its destruction is not possible. Just as capitalism cannot exist without a non-capitalist society, civilisation as the official world system cannot exist without the existence of the democratic civilisation system. More concretely, the civilisation with monopoly could not exist without the civilisation with no monopoly. The opposite of this is not true. In other words, democratic civilisation, the historical flow of moral and political society, could exist quite comfortably and be more free from obstruction without official civilisation. I define democratic civilisation as a thought system and accumulation of thought, as well as a totality of moral rules and political organs.

We conceptualised the political dimension of the KCK's construction of the democratic nation as democratic autonomy. Without self-governance the democratic nation is unthinkable. In general, all forms of nations, and particularly democratic nations, are societal entities that have their own self-governance. If a society is deprived of self-governance, it ceases to be a nation. The Kurds were not only prevented from becoming a nation, they also ceased to exist as a society. The guidance by the PKK and the policies of the KCK not only stopped this process, but also initiated the process of becoming a democratic nation rather than a political society. Kurds, at their current stage, are not only a society that has become intensely political, but a society that also works to transform this political reality into a democratic nation.

The KCK plays a key role in the construction of the democratic nation and may be translated as the equivalent of democratic autonomy. The KCK's fulfilment of its role as the organ for democratic politics is indispensable in the creation of a democratic nation. To confuse it with a nation-state is a deliberate distortion. The KCK, as a principle, has ceased to employ nation-statism as a tool for finding a solution. It is neither the first nor the last stage of nation-statism. They are both qualitatively different concepts of authority. Although it may contain features that are reminiscent of the nation-states' institutionalisation in terms of its organisational structure, it is quintessentially different. KONGRA-GEL,[2] as the KCK's decision-making body, means People's Assembly. Its importance is derived from people making their own decisions themselves. The People's Assembly is a democratic organ. It is the alternative to becoming a nation governed by the upper classes or the bourgeoisie. KONGRA-GEL signifies becoming a nation governed by the popular classes and stratum of intellectuals. It is essentially different from the bourgeois parliamentarian system. The Executive Council of the KCK expresses the condensed and centralised daily administration pyramid. It ensures coordination between the

---

2   The People's Congress of Kurdistan was formed in 2003 and is the legislative organ of the KCK.

working units scattered among the people. It coordinates the daily organisational-operational work involved in becoming a democratic nation as well as governing and defending it. The Council should not be confused with government organs of the state. It is closer to the system of confederations of democratic civil societies. The KCK's General Presidential Institution, resting on election by the people, is the most general and highest level of representation. It supervises and monitors the compatibility between all the KCK's units and the application of fundamental policies.

It is clear that during such a period and under new conditions there will be considerable competition, contention and conflict between the nation-states' institutions and forces and the KCK's institutions and forces. There will be different authorities and governances in the cities and rural areas.

SOCIAL LIFE

In the process of becoming a democratic nation, important transformations occur in social life. Traditional life in capitalist modernity undergoes great changes.

The dominant modern lifestyle has turned into a complete trap based around the oldest slave, the woman. In capitalism, women have been turned into the 'queens of commodity'. They are not only unwaged workers, as 'housewives', they are the lowest wage earners outside of the house and the main tool for lowering wages.

The woman is the foremost constituent of flexible employment. She is an industrial incubator producing the new generations required by the capitalist system. She is the principal tool for the advertising industry. Her servitude perpetuates sexism. From the global to the little emperor in the family, she is the instrument of unlimited pleasure and power of all dominant men. She is the object that gives birth to the power of those who never had power. At no point in history has the woman been exploited as much as she has been during capitalist modernity. All other slaveries – child and male slavery – have developed in the footsteps of women's enslavement. This is why in the social life imposed by capitalism everyone, except for those who rule, has been infantilised as much as enslaved. The family, which is shaped around the woman and is the oldest institution of society, is disintegrating yet again around the woman. What disintegrates the family is capitalism's manner of accumulation. This manner can only materialise itself as it consumes society, and the expected result is that society can be consumed and atomised in so far as it is able to destroy the fundamental cell of the society: the family.

No matter how much the field of medicine develops, it is unable to stop the rapid spread of disease within society. Nationalism, religionism, powerism and sexism are the cognitive and emotional DNA of capitalism, constantly generating diseases both individually and institutionally. The increasing number of inherent illnesses is an indicator of mental and psychological disease – the inevitable outcome of capitalism's destructive effect on society.

In modern social life, the education system is responsible for the creation of the anti-social individual. Both the liberal individualist life and the life of the nation-statist citizen are programmed and implemented in accordance with the requirements of capitalism. For this purpose, a huge industry called the education sector has been formed. In this sector, individuals are bombarded 24 hours a day both mentally and spiritually in order to be turned into anti-social beings. They are prevented from becoming moral and political. They are turned into individuals who are compelled to consume, who run after money, are sexist, chauvinist and lickspittle. This is how social nature is destroyed. Education is not used to enhance the healthy functioning of society, but to destroy it.

A democratic nation is above all adamant about remaining a society; it stands against capitalist modernity with the slogan 'society or nothing'. It insists on the sustenance of society as a historical-social reality, although the society is dissolved within the grindstones of modernity.

Because the democratic nation's understanding of education targets sociality and the free individual-citizen, the dialectic of the development of the individual with the society and society's development with the individual is re-established. The socialising, liberating and equalising role of the sciences is reaffirmed. Democratic nation is the nationhood of a society that has acquired a true awareness of its existence.

FREE PARTNER LIFE

We know that there are three main functions for all living organisms: nutrition, self-preservation and preservation of the species. These fundamental functions take on a new level in humans.

Once the consciousness of the desire to live is attained, it should also be understood that through procreation alone one can not grasp the meaning of life. Just as reproduction does not make life meaningful, it might even distort and weaken the emergent power of consciousness. Having awareness of one's own self is undoubtedly an amazing thing to happen in the universe. Ascribing divinity to human beings was not in vain. Continuing the bloodline of the conscious human not only impairs the balance, to the detriment of other living beings, it also endangers humanity's power of consciousness. In short, the main problem of the conscious human cannot be the continuation of its bloodline. If, as far as we know, the universe has achieved the highest level of power – to know itself within the human being for the very first time – then this is something worth getting excited about. Maybe understanding the universe is the true meaning of life. This, in turn, would mean that the life–death cycle has been transcended; there could be no greater source of excitement and rejoicing for humanity.

The most important result of the PKK's revolutionary people's war in relation to male chauvinism is its understanding that the liberation and freedom of society is only possible through the analysis of the phenomenon of woman, as well as her liberation and freedom. However, as has been pointed out, the Kurdish male mistakenly defines his so-called honour in terms of his absolute sovereignty over women. This egregious contradiction needs to be resolved.

On the way to building a democratic nation, we will have to do the opposite of what has been done to date in the name of honour. I am talking about a transformed Kurdish manhood, and in part I am talking about myself. It should be done like this: we must abandon any notion of ownership in relation to women. Woman should only belong to herself (*xwebûn*). She should know that she has no owner, and that the only owner she has is herself. We should not be attached to women with any emotions of subordination, including love and blind love. Likewise, the woman too should stop herself from being dependent and owned. This should be the first condition of being a revolutionary, a militant. Those who come through this experience successfully, are those who realise freedom in their personality, and who can build the new society and democratic nation starting with their own liberated personalities.

The liberation of women is very important in the process of becoming a democratic nation. The liberation of women is the liberation of society. The society that becomes free, on the other hand, is a democratic nation. I talked about the revolutionary significance of reversing the role of the man. This means, instead of approaching the woman as a means of continuing his bloodline or dominating her, he should sustain the process of becoming a democratic nation through his own strength – he should form the ideological and organisational power needed for this, and should ensure the sovereignty of his own political authority; thus he should ideologically and politically produce himself. Therefore, rather than physical reproduction, he must ensure spiritual and intellectual empowerment. Capitalist modernity is a system based on the denial of love. The denial of society, the uncontrollability of individualism, pervasive sexism, the deification of money, the substitution of nation-state for God and the transformation of women into unwaged or low-paid workers also mean denial of the material basis of love.

The female nature must be understood clearly. To approach a woman's sexuality solely by finding her biologically attractive, and to relate to her on this basis, is the loss of love from the very beginning. Just as we don't call the biological mating of other species love, we cannot call biologically based sexual intercourse between humans love either. We can call this the normal breeding activity of living beings. There is no need to be human to conduct these activities. Those who want true love have to abandon this animal-human type of reproduction. We can see women as valuable friends and comrades only to the extent that we transcend viewing them as objects of sexual appeal. The most difficult relationship is one of friendship and camaraderie with a woman that transcends sexism. Even when life is freely shared with a woman as a partner, the building of society and democratic nation should form its basis. We must overcome the traditional boundaries, and as in modernity, of seeing women only in the roles of partners, mothers, sisters or lovers. First and foremost, we must forge strong human relationships based on a common understanding and the building of society. If a man wants to have a relationship with a woman that has a strong ideological and societal foundation, then he needs to leave the choice and the courting to the woman. The more a woman's level of freedom, ability to choose freely, and mobility based on her own strength have developed, the more one can live with her meaningfully and beautifully.

We continuously emphasise that the conditions under which *jin* and *jiyan* cease to be woman and life reflect the collapse and disintegration of the society. Without this reality being understood and acted on, it is impossible for those components that we call revolution, revolutionary party, guides and militants to play their role. It is impossible for those who are themselves in a deadlock to solve other peoples' deadlocks and to make them free. The most important consequence of the PKK and its revolutionary people's warfare in this regard is that the liberation and freedom of society can only be achieved through the analysis of the phenomenon of woman, and her liberation and freedom.

ECONOMIC AUTONOMY

The nation-state is the instrument with which capitalist modernity establishes its control over an economy that rests on realising maximum profits. Without this instrument, maximising profits and capital accumulation cannot be achieved. It represents the highest level of economic plunder, while maintaining a certain amount of legitimacy, in the history of civilisation. A correct definition of the nation-state cannot be made without analysing its relationship to maximising profits and capital accumulation. The nation-state cannot be defined solely as a system of tyranny and power either. Only when state power is organised as a nation-state can capitalist modernity and, in particular, its maximum profit and capital accumulation over the economy be realised. This means that the nation-state's control over the economic life of society has allowed the state to seize more surplus value than ever. It is coated with the varnish of nationalism and patriotism, deified through education, and it penetrates society completely to legitimise the economic extortion it has perpetrated. Concepts, theories and institutions developed in the fields of law, political economy and diplomacy all pursue legitimacy with the same objective. The enforcement of a relentless terror, together with the attainment of maximum profit, on the one hand condemns society to minimum waged labour, while on the other hand it transforms the majority into an army of the unemployed. Low-wage slavery and an enormous army of the unemployed are the natural consequences of the drive to maximise profits, the nation-state and industrialism.

The realisation of these three fundamental components of capitalist modernity is only made possible when society loses control and the freedom to make choices over its economic life, and is condemned to waged slavery, with the majority of the population transformed into an army of the unemployed, and women condemned to unpaid or low-wage slavery. Capitalism's social sciences in general, and in particular its political economy, are mythologies concocted to conceal and distort these facts; one must never believe them and must know what these myths entail.

Kurdish society is a society that has been frightened to stand up for itself as a consequence of the cultural genocide it has endured through conquests, occupations, invasions, looting, colonialism and assimilation, as well as the consequences of capitalist modernity. It is a society that has lost control over its own economy and has been taken under the complete control of the three-legged modern monster of foreign and collaborationist elements. The fact that it only works to feed itself shows that it is a society that has been tied down to genocidal intent. It is a society in which women, the creators of economy, are rendered unemployed and their labour considered of least value. It is a society whose men have been scattered across the world in search of work in order to support their families. It is a society in which people kill each other for a chicken or a plot of land. Clearly, such a society has ceased to be a society and is one that has crumbled and dissolved.

Economic occupation is the most dangerous of all occupations. It is the most barbaric way to degrade and destroy a society. More than the suppression and tyranny of the nation-state, Kurdish society has been eviscerated by the loss of its economic tools and of control over its economic domain. It is not possible for a society to maintain its freedom once it has lost control over its means of production and its market. The Kurds have not only effectively lost control over their means and relations of production; they have also lost control over their production, consumption and trade. More precisely, it was only possible for them to make use of their property, and partake in trade and industry, in so far as they attached themselves to sovereign nation-states through relinquishing their identities. Economic captivity was an effective tool in the denial of identity and loss of freedom. The unilateral enterprises established over the rivers and oil reservoirs have not only destroyed ancient cultural artefacts but also much fertile land. The intensification of economic colonialism which came after political and cultural colonisation was the final nail in the coffin. The final point arrived at is: 'either cease to be a society, or die!'

The economic system of a democratic nation not only puts a stop to these barbaric practices, it bases itself on society re-establishing control over its own economy. Economic autonomy is the minimum compromise to be reached between the nation-state and democratic nation; any lesser compromise is a mandate for surrender and annihilation. The furthering of economic autonomy to independence would mean establishing an opposing nation-state, which is ultimately surrendering to capitalist modernity. Relinquishing economic autonomy, on the other hand, would mean surrendering to the dominant nation-state. The essence of economic autonomy predicates neither private capitalism nor state capitalism. It is predicated on ecological industry and communal economy – the form where democracy is reflected in the economy. Industry, development, technology, businesses and ownership are bound by the principle of being an ecological and democratic society. In economic autonomy there is no room for industry, technology, development, ownership or rural-urban settlement that negate ecological and democratic society. The economy cannot be left as a domain where profit and capital accumulation materialises.

Economic autonomy is a model in which profit and capital accumulation is minimised. Although it does not reject the market, trade, product variety, competition and productivity, it does, however, reject the dominance of profit and capital accumulation. Finance and financial systems are validated only insofar as they serve economic productivity and functionality. Making money from money is regarded as the most effortless form of exploitation, which has no place in economic autonomy. The economic autonomy of a democratic nation does not regard work as drudgery, but as an act of liberation. To see work as drudgery is to be alienated from the results of labour. When the results of labour serve one's own identity and the individual's freedom, the situation changes for the better. This isn't the same as real socialism's efforts towards collectivisation. In the commune, there is no place for drudgery or for work and labour that are not liberating.

The dams built on Kurdistan's rivers have led to historical genocide and ecological disaster. No dam that ignores ecology, fertile land or history can be permitted; even those that have already been built will not be replaced when they decay. If possible, early elimination should not be avoided. Opposition to deforestation and erosion – the biggest enemy of society and life – chimes with the spirit of total mobilisation. It declares the protection of land and reforestation to be the most valuable forms of labour.

The KCK, as the backbone of the democratic nation, predicates itself on and sees economic autonomy and communal economy as essential to the self-defence of society. Just as society cannot sustain itself without self-defence, the nourishment and sustenance of society is only possible with economic autonomy, dependent on soil conservation and reforestation, ecology and commune.

Economic autonomy also requires a legal basis. The uniformity and centralism of the laws of the sovereign nation-state hamper economic creativity, the environment and competition under the pretext of unity. In place of such an understanding of law based on economic colonialism, there is an urgent need for a localised economy that functions autonomously but which takes into account coordination with the national economy. An economic law that makes allowance for local market dynamics, but which does not deny the national market, is crucial. A single, central legal system is the most important factor underpinning conservatism. It is completely political and makes no economic sense.

LEGAL STRUCTURE

Democratic law is a law based on diversity. More importantly, it makes little reference to legal regulation and is a simple construct. Throughout history, the sovereign nation-state is a state form that has developed legal regulations to the greatest extent, in order to eliminate moral and political society. Past societies largely attempted to solve their problems through moral and political regulations. Capitalist modernity has attempted to base all of its legitimacy on law. Capitalist modernity's excessive intervention in and exploitation of society led it to resort to a complicated tool called law that formalised justice.

Law, rather than consisting of laws regulating the rights and duties of individuals and society, as it is so often claimed to be, is the art of ruling through excessive regulation intended to legitimise the injustices caused by capitalism. Ruling through laws rather than moral and political rules is specific to capitalist modernity. Rejecting morals and politics, the bourgeoisie resorts to the instrument of law, which gives it enormous power. In the hands of the bourgeoisie, law is a powerful weapon. It defends itself through law against both the former moral and political order and the workers. The power of the nation-state is largely derived from the power of a legal system that has been unilaterally regulated. The laws, in a sense, are the verses of the nation-state god. It prefers to rule its society through these verses.

It is for this reason that the democratic nation is sensitive towards law, especially constitutional law. The democratic nation is more of a moral and political nation than a nation based on law. The need for law arises if a life with nation-states under a common political roof and compromise is opted for. When this happens, the distinction between national law and the laws of local government gains importance. When the nation-state laws, which are based on unilaterally centralised bureaucratic interests, constantly face the resistance of local and cultural democratic groups they must embrace the laws of the local government.

Due to the fact that the existence of Kurdistan and the Kurds has been denied, the Kurds have no laws specific to them. During the Ottoman period, the Kurds had both written and traditional laws. From 1925 onwards, Kurdish identity was regarded as non-existent, to be wiped from history through conspiracies, coups and assimilation. While the PKK's resistance has re-established the existence of the Kurds, it has not yet been able to ensure a legal definition. The KCK will work to persuade nation-states to recognise the Kurdish entity legally, but if this does not happen it will unilaterally develop its own autonomous legal system. However, the KCK will prioritise finding a place for itself within other national constitutions, working to express its democratic autonomy status within them. This is what is meant by a peaceful and democratic solution to the Kurdish question: national democratic constitutional compromise based on democratic autonomy status. If the KCK does not succeed in its preferred national democratic constitutional solution with democratic autonomy status based on a compromise, it will make the transition to unilateral democratic autonomous governance as its second preferred option. The democratic autonomous governance in Kurdistan is not a nation-state with governance through laws. It is the governance of democratic modernity on a local and regional scale.

CULTURE

The state rests on thousands of years of patriarchal culture. The state institution is a male invention, where wars with the objective of pillaging and looting have almost become a form of production. Instead of woman's social effectivity based on production, a transition to man's social effectivity based on wars and booty occurred. There is a close correlation between the enslavement of women and warrior society culture. War does not produce, it seizes and pillages. Although in certain specific circumstances violence has played a decisive role in societal development – clearing the path to freedom, and resisting occupation, invasion and colonialism – it is largely destructive and negative. The internalised culture of violence in a society is also fuelled by wars. The sword of war among states and the hand of man within the family both epitomise domination.

In addition, by formalising the cultural norms of a dominant ethnicity or a religious community under the name of national culture, capitalist modernity declares war against all other cultural entities. By claiming that religions, ethnicities, peoples, nations, languages and cultures that have preserved themselves for thousands of years 'harm national unity', capitalist modernity prepares to destroy them either by force or through material incentives. In no other time in history have so many languages, religions, denominations, ethnic tribes and *aşiret* (a federation of tribal communities), as well as peoples and nations, fallen victim to these policies, or to be more precise, genocides. Physical genocides are actually a drop in the ocean when compared with immaterial genocide. Cultural and linguistic values together with communities that have existed for thousands of years are sacrificed, for the sake of the sacred act of creating 'national unity'.

The cultural dimension, too, is important in the formation of nations. In a narrow sense, culture represents the traditional mentality and emotional reality of a society. Again, in a narrow sense, religion, philosophy, mythology, science and various art forms constitute the culture of a society. In a way, they represent the mindset and mental state of a society. In a nation-state, or as nations are formed by the state, the world of culture is greatly distorted and decimated. This is because in no other way can the state legitimise its rule of maximum profit and capital accumulation. Modernity and the nation-state cannot develop without first reconstructing culture and history according to their own interests. The resulting reality of modernity and the nation-state has no relation to the reality of history and culture; it represents a different meaning in terms of the truth.

The role of culture in capitalist modernity is vital. Culture, as the total mentality of all social spheres, is first subjected to assimilation (to accommodate economic and political hegemony), then it is turned into an industry to be spread extensively and intensively to all societies (nations, peoples, nation-states, civil society, corporations) of the world. The industrialisation of culture is the second most effective means of enslavement. Culture, in a narrow sense, represents the mindset of societies. Thought, taste and morals are its three fundamental issues. It has taken centuries for political and economic power to besiege and buy off cultural elements. They have regarded the appropriation of cultural elements as indispensable for their legitimacy throughout civilisational history. Economic and ruling powers were quick to notice this and to take precautions. The assimilation of culture by rulers dates back to the inception of hierarchy. It is the essential tool for ruling. Without cultural hegemony, economic and power monopolies cannot rule. The empire stage of capitalism is only possible with a developed cultural industry. It is for this reason that the struggle against cultural hegemony requires constant diligence.

In contrast, democratic society, moral and political society's contemporary form of modernity, is a society that truly accommodates difference in the broadest sense. All social groups within democratic society can coexist on the basis of differences that form around their own culture and identity without being confined to a uniform culture and citizenship. Communities can reveal their potential in these differences, whether they are political or in terms of identity, and transform it into an active life. None of the communities have any concern that they would be homogenised. Uniformity is seen as deformity, poverty-stricken and boring. Pluriformity, however, offers richness, beauty and tolerance. Freedom and equality flourish under these conditions. Only equality and freedom that rest on diversity are valuable. As a matter of fact, freedom and equality attained via the nation-states is only for monopolies, as proven around the world. Power and capital monopolies never allow true freedoms or equality. Freedom and equality can only be acquired through the democratic politics of democratic society, and protected with self-defence.

Just as it is possible to bring together different ethnic cultures within the scope of the democratic nation, it is also important to utilise the democratic content of religious culture within the democratic nation as a free, equal and democratic component, and allow room for it in a resolution. The reconciliatory alliance approach developed by democratic modernity towards all anti-systemic movements should also be developed towards religious culture with democratic content; this is within the scope of another task that is of vital importance. The democratic nation tries to compose itself by reinstating the true meaning of history and culture, which in the process is reborn in the formation of the democratic nation.

The democratic nation solution to the Kurdish question is first and foremost linked to the correct definition of Kurdish history and culture. The correct definition of its history and culture will bring recognition of its social existence. The denial and annihilation of the Kurds in the Republic of Turkey's history began with the denial of Kurdish history and the annihilation of its cultural heritage, first eliminating its immaterial culture and then its material culture. It is for this reason that it was right for the PKK to begin building with an awareness of history and culture. By attempting to explain Kurdish history and culture through comparison with other people's history and culture around the world, and to proclaim it in a manifesto called *The Path of the Kurdistan Revolution*, allowed the PKK to play the role of a revolutionary renaissance in the reinvigoration of Kurdish history and culture.

The construction of the Kurdish democratic nation is qualitatively different from nationalist and statist nation-building processes. It is different from sovereign nation-state nationalism and Kurdish nationalist and statist approaches; it is an alternative construction of a nation grounded on the history and culture of workers and peoples.

The Kurdish democratic nation will gradually acquire a further structural quality under the KCK, and present a new praxis of nation construction that will become a model for the Middle Eastern peoples. It is open to more extensive democratic national unions and alliances with other peoples on the basis of an open-ended understanding of democratic nationhood. It will initiate the rise of a new era, the era of democratic modernity, through the revolutionary and democratic nation renaissance against the cultural and historical denialism of nation-states that cannot transcend their role as agents of Western modernity.

SELF-DEFENCE SYSTEM

All species of living organisms have defence systems of their own. There is not a single defenceless species. As a matter of fact, it is possible to interpret the resistance shown by each element or particle in the universe to protect its existence as self-defence.

The same system is more than valid for the human species and their societies. Defence in humans is as much social as it is biological. Biological defence is performed by the defensive instincts of every living organism. In societal defence, however, all the individuals of the community collectively defend themselves. Moreover, the number of communities and their organisational form constantly change according to the means of defence. Defence is an essential function of society. Life cannot be sustained without it.

Another important conclusion we can draw from the self-defence mechanisms of living organisms is that this defence is only intended for the protection of their existence. They do not establish dominance and colonisation systems over their own species or any other species. Systems of domination and exploitation were first developed by the human species. The mental development of the human species that resulted in possibilities of exploitation, and in connection with this the attainment of surplus product, plays a role here. This situation leads to human beings protecting their existence along with defending the values of labour – in other words, social wars.

When we view things from the democratic society perspective, we must underline the following: when we talk about self-defence rather than a military stance or an armed organisation what we mean is the organisation of society to protect itself in every sphere, and for it to struggle based on these organisations. This said, in order to counter the attacks from the statist system against society and to protect society, military organisations may also be needed to defend society in all its diversity. This could be deemed as legitimate defence. But this sort of military organisation, organised in this way, serving to protect society and its reorganisation, cannot merely be evaluated as a military organisation. The function of the military forces at the service of society, the fundamental self-defence forces, is to play the role of a catalyst to speed up and protect the struggle of democratic society. Military forces that move away from these functions cannot avoid being transformed into offensive forces that are instruments of hegemonic tendencies.

Self-defence does not only stipulate an armed structure; although it does not reject the use of force when necessary, it cannot be viewed only as an armed structure. It represents the organisation of society in all spheres and in relation to its own identity and life: the decisions taken to this end reflect society's own will and are implemented at society's behest. Values that used to belong to the people and the country but were usurped by colonialist powers are retrieved and returned to social values in an act of self-defence. Society should attain a position where it can both protect its values and recover its usurped rights in order for it to govern itself. This is the way to create a democratic nation.

A self-defence mechanism for women, as the most oppressed and suppressed segment of society, is also of vital importance. Under the patriarchal system all rights of women were usurped. Women can circumvent these policies of degradation, harassment, rape and slaughter through the formation of their own self-defence mechanisms. For this reason, they need to learn their history, create their own organisations and institutions, carve out space for themselves in all areas of life and if necessary create their own military forces.

An important and indispensable heading within the KCK's programme for the construction of a democratic nation is how self-defence is going to be tied to a permanent, systematic mechanism. The nation-states, the sole armed monopolies, will be unsparing if they have the opportunity to implement new policies of denial, annihilation and assimilation. These policies have compelled the creation of a permanent self-defence system by the KCK. The minimum requirement for coexistence with nation-states is for Kurdish identity and existence to be constitutionally guaranteed. Constitutional guarantee is not enough: concrete grounds for this guarantee should be sought through statuses determined by law. Apart from the joint national defence for external threats, Kurdish society should meet its own security requirements. This is because a society can only ensure its internal security in accordance with its requirements. Therefore, the related nation-states (the centralised nation-states of Turkey, Iran, Iraq and Syria) must implement important reforms of their own internal security policies.

If a compromise cannot be agreed with the relevant nation-states, the KCK, on the basis of protecting the unilateral construction of the democratic nation with all its dimensions, should try to organise the quantitative and qualitative status of its own self-defence forces according to new needs.

DIPLOMACY

One of the most developed activities by the nation-state is diplomacy between nation-states. Diplomacy describes pre-war activities between nation-states. It may even be defined as the preparatory phase for wars in the history of nation-states. Throughout history there have always been certain rituals of expressing neighbourhood relations between different types of communal units. These are deemed to be valuable. The reason nation-states have institutionalised this relationship can be linked to the profit tendency of capitalist modernity. If relationships are more profitable in times of peace then there is no need for war. Diplomacy serves to achieve profitable relations. If the maximum profit tendency is linked to war, then diplomatic forces will be unable to avert a profitable war, thus terminating the need for diplomacy. Diplomacy has been reduced to the logic of profit; it no longer has any link to the meaningful intersocietal relations that have existed throughout history. Diplomacy has been degraded to a manipulative tool in the game of profitable wars between nation-states.

Democratic nation diplomacy must first create a common platform between Kurds who are fragmented and divided in various ways. All other diplomatic activities, especially those that each organisation wishes to develop on their own and according to their own interests, have done more harm than good and have served to fragment, create conflict and divide Kurds further. It is for this reason that establishing the Democratic National Congress is the most vital priority for Kurdish diplomacy. Diplomacy that rests on the

Iraqi-Kurdish Federal State is important, but cannot meet the needs of all Kurdish people. This state has neither the ability to meet this demand nor the conditions that would allow it to do so. A diplomacy that meets the needs of all Kurds can be developed only through a Democratic National Congress. Therefore, the primary task is to assemble the Democratic National Congress and declare it to be a permanent general integrative national democratic organisation. It is clear that for some time to come, relations and contradictions both ideologically and politically will continue between the KCK as it builds a democratic nation and the Kurdistan Regional Government in Iraq's nation-statist construction. In this regard, the Democratic National Congress may serve as a solution-oriented umbrella organisation.

Diplomacy, which once again becomes a tool for peace and solidarity as well as creative exchanges between societies, deals essentially with solutions to problems. Democratic nation diplomacy is a tool for peace and beneficial relations, not wars. It signifies a mission where wise people play a role and which has high ethical and political values. It plays an important role in developing and maintaining bilaterally beneficial processes and friendly relations, especially among neighbouring peoples and related communities. It is the constructive force of common socialities and the synthesis of societies at higher levels. The diplomacy of the democratic nation can play a lasting role and provide solutions in the context of democratic modernity between the peoples and nations of the Middle East who have endured chaos and conflict because of nation-state diplomacy. The global union of democratic nations, as an alternative to the UN, is the World Confederation of Democratic Nations. Continents and large cultural regions can form their own Confederations of Democratic Nations, too.

TO BE A SEEKER OF A DEMOCRATIC NATION SOLUTION

The construction of a democratic nation in Kurdistan is the new historical and societal expression of Kurdish existence and its free life, which requires both theoretical and practical concentration and transformation. It represents a truth that requires devotion at the level of real love. Just as there is no room for false love on this voyage, there is also no room for uncommitted travellers. On this voyage, the question of when the construction of the democratic nation will be completed is a redundant one. This is a construction that will never be finished: it is an ongoing process. The construction of a democratic nation has the freedom to recreate itself at every instant. In societal terms, there can be no utopia or reality that is more ambitious than this. In accordance with their historical and societal reality, the Kurds have vigorously turned towards the construction of a democratic nation. As a matter of fact, they have lost nothing by ridding themselves of a nation-state god in which they never believed; they are free of a heavy burden, a burden that brought them to the brink of annihilation. Instead, they have gained the opportunity to become a democratic nation.

The Kurds, as individuals and as a society, must conceive, internalise and implement the construction of a democratic nation as the synthesis of all expressions of truth and resistance throughout their history, including the most ancient goddess beliefs, Zoroastrianism and Islam. The truths that all the past mythological, religious and philosophical teachings, as well as contemporary social sciences, have tried to teach, and that all resistance wars and rebellions have individually and collectively tried to voice, are represented in the mind and body of constructing a democratic nation. It was this reality and its expression as truth that was my point of departure, not only when I periodically recreated myself, but especially on arriving at the present as I tried to recreate myself at almost every instant. In this way I have freely socialised myself, concretised this as a democratic nation (in a Kurdish context) and presented it as democratic modernity to all humanity, to the oppressed peoples and individuals of the Middle East.

It is clear that care needs to be taken in order to prevent liberalism – as it so often has done throughout its history – from degenerating and dissolving these positive tendencies of democratisation under its own ideological and material hegemony. The most strategic task is to unify not only all system opponents but also the flow of historical society, with all its urbanist, local and regional political formations in a new ideological and political structure. In this regard, intertwined with comprehensive theoretical work that needs to be taken up, there is a need to develop a programme and structures for organisation and action. The conditions are ripe in the twenty-first century to avoid the fate of confederal structures which were eliminated by the nation-states in the mid-nineteenth century, and to achieve the victory of democratic confederalism. In order for democratic modernity to come out of this deepest and longest lasting crisis, sustained only through crisis management during modernity's financial capital era, the ability to succeed in the intellectual, moral and political duties of reconstruction has never had such a vital significance.

CONCLUSION

If new parties standing for freedom and equality want to be consistent, then they must develop politics and social forms that are not centred around the state. The alternative to the state is democracy. All paths – aside from democracy – that have been attempted in efforts to counter the state have come to nothing. Contrary to popular belief, democracy is not a form of capitalist state. In addition, nothing other than democracy can restrict the state and keep it within the law. To topple a state doesn't mean you have overcome state culture. A new one can always be created to fill the vacuum. Only democracy shares the same area as the state; by restricting the state, it widens society's sphere of freedom. It can thus approach equality more closely by reducing the number of appropriated values.

Therefore, we can define democracy as the self-governance of a non-state society. Democracy is governance that is not state; it is the power of communities to govern themselves without the state. Contrary to popular belief, since its formation human society has experienced democracy more than it has experienced the state.

Perhaps the situation of a general country or nation's democracy has not been intensely experienced. But the emergence of society's existence is communal and democratic. Without communality, or in the absence of having a democratic reflex, it is impossible for a society to be solely ruled by the state. The state can only rule by growing at the expense of communality and democracy. The grounds out of which the state rises and on which it thrives are the society's communality – the need for coexistence – and democratic stance. There is a dialectic relationship between the two. Therefore, when society and civilisation meet, the main contradiction is between the state and democracy. Less of one is more of the other. Full democracy is statelessness. Full state sovereignty is the denial of democracy. States can only be toppled by states; democracy does not topple the state, it can only pave the way for a newer state like real socialism did. Democracy's fundamental function becomes evident in this manner. It can only increase the opportunities for freedom and equality by restricting the state, making it smaller and by trimming its octopus-like tentacles and their power over society. Towards the end of the process, perhaps the state will become redundant and fizzle out. The conclusion we draw from this is that the relationship between the state and democracy is not of one toppling another, but of transcendence.

What I am trying to show with this short analysis is that the PKK's worldview has contained a fundamental mistake from the beginning it being a state-oriented party. These parties, whether they form a state or not, cannot achieve their objectives of democracy, freedom and equality through state formation. Without deviating from this path, one cannot become a new libertarian and egalitarian party. In short, the way to become a democratic and socialist party is to ensure renewal by making the transition from a state-oriented theory, programme, strategy and tactics. There is a need for a non-state-oriented democratic socialist theory, programme, strategy and tactics. If self-criticism develops within this context, it will be meaningful. Otherwise, the old methods will persist under the guise of the new. The state of real socialism, social democracy and national liberation parties is enough to prove this reality.

Just as it has been the case many times throughout history between civilisational forces and democratic forces, capitalist modernity forces and democratic modernity forces can accept the existence and identity of one another, and can coexist peacefully on the basis of recognising democratic autonomous governances. Within this scope and under these conditions, within and outside the borders of a nation-state, democratic confederal political formations can peacefully coexist with nation-state formations.

I have tried to puzzle out and comprehensively analyse the proposition that while capitalist modernity survives on the basis of capitalism, industrialism and nation-statism, democratic modernity can only come into existence through democratic communality, ecological industry and a democratic nation. I have defined democratic communality not as the egalitarianism of a homogeneous society, but as any type of community (from women's to men's communities, from sports and arts to industry, from intellectuals to shepherds, from tribes to corporations, from families to nations, from villages to cities, from localities to universality, and from clan to any type of global society) of any size. I defined eco-industrial communities as communities in which the eco-industrial society, the agricultural society of villages and the industrial society of the cities nurture each other and are strictly aligned with ecology. On the other hand I also defined the democratic nation. It is a new type of nation that encompasses all cultural entities, from ethnicity to religion, from urban, local and regional to national communities formed through democratic autonomous political formations and its main political form: democratic confederalist implementations. More precisely, against the nation-statist monsters, the democratic nation is a nation that has multi-political formations, multiple identities and is multicultural.

As we try to analyse the last 5,000 years of civilisational history in terms of the two conflicting poles, we understand that these two poles will continue to coexist for some time to come. The eradication of one of the poles by the other is not foreseeable in the near future. Moreover, dialectically this does not seem realistic. The rashness of real socialism in this regard, and its attempt to try implementing its own system without first analysing civilisation and modernity, resulted in its own dissolution. The important thing is to take into account this bipolarity in all theoretical and practical work, and continuously to develop democratic civilisation and modernity within daily life and through new constructive work. The more we develop our system through both revolutionary and evolutionary methods, the more we can positively solve the problems of *term* and *space* and make the solution permanent. Democratic modernity as a system, including its fundamental elements, is well suited for true peace. The democratic nation, with its clear ability to create solutions from the smallest national community through to a world nation, offers a very valuable peace option.

The important thing is to institutionalise the communal and democratic identity, which is also the basic stance of peoples historically, with contemporary science and technological resources by unifying them. In order to have a more democratic, liberated and ecological social structure, there is a need above all for a new social sciences structure. It should not be forgotten that the most comprehensive and permanent component of democratisation is women's freedom. Without the attainment of societal gender equality, no demand for freedom or equality can be meaningful or realised.

Nowadays, democracy is needed, just like bread, air and water, but nowhere more so than for the peoples of the Middle East. There is no other option but democracy – all others have been tested throughout history – which has the ability to bring happiness to the people. The Kurds are at the forefront of these peoples. If they can successfully mobilise their geography, historical time and societal characteristics – all of which have become significant strategic elements – in favour of democratic civilisation in the Middle East, they will have done the greatest good for their neighbours and for humanity. What we have undertaken is a draft of this noble and exciting task.

Index

Abdullah Öcalan led the Kurdish liberation struggle as the head of the PKK from its foundation in 1978 until his abduction in 1999. He is still regarded as a leading strategist and the most important political representative of the Kurdish people. Under isolation conditions at Imrali Island Prison, Öcalan authored more than ten books.